The Triangle Shirtwaist Company Fire of 1911

The Triangle Shirtwaist Company Fire of 1911

Gina De Angelis

CHELSEA HOUSE PUBLISHERS
Philadelphia

Dedicated to the memory of Giovanni, Carmella, Domenico, Genoveffa, Donato, and Yolanda, who dreamed of a better life in America and made it come true.

CHELSEA HOUSE PUBLISHERS

Editor in Chief Stephen Reginald
Production Manager Pamela Loos
Art Director Sara Davis
Director of Photography Judy L. Hasday
Managing Editor James D. Gallagher
Senior Production Editor J. Christopher Higgins

Staff for THE TRIANGLE SHIRTWAIST COMPANY FIRE OF 1911

Senior Editor LeeAnne Gelletly
Associate Art Director Takeshi Takahashi
Picture Researcher Patricia Burns
Cover Illustrator/Designer Keith Trego

First Printing

1 3 5 7 9 8 6 4 2

The Chelsea House World Wide Web address is
http://www.chelseahouse.com

Library of Congress Cataloging-in-Publication Data

De Angelis, Gina.
The Triangle Shirtwaist Company fire of 1911 / Gina De Angelis.
    p. cm -- (Great disasters)
Includes bibliographical references (p.) and index.
Summary: Examines, using eyewitness accounts, the tragedy that killed 146 workers in a New York City garment factory.

ISBN 0-7910-5267-2

1. Triangle Shirtwaist Company—Fire, 1911—Juvenile literature. 2. New York (N.Y.)—History—1898-1951—Juvenile literature. 3. Clothing factories—New York (State)—New York—Safety measures—History—20th century—Juvenile literature. [1. Triangle Shirtwaist Company—Fire, 1911.] I. Title. II. Great disasters and their reforms.
F128.5 D43 2000
974.7'1—dc21   99-086848

Contents

GREAT DISASTERS
REFORMS and RAMIFICATIONS

Jill McCaffrey
National Chairman
Armed Forces Emergency Services
American Red Cross

Introduction

Disasters have always been a source of fascination and awe. Tales of a great flood that nearly wipes out all life are among humanity's oldest recorded stories, dating at least from the second millennium B.C., and they appear in cultures from the Middle East to the Arctic Circle to the southernmost tip of South America and the islands of Polynesia. Typically gods are at the center of these ancient disaster tales—which is perhaps not too surprising, given the fact that the tales originated during a time when human beings were at the mercy of natural forces they did not understand.

To a great extent, we still are at the mercy of nature, as anyone who reads the newspapers or watches nightly news broadcasts can attest. Hurricanes, earthquakes, tornados, wildfires, and floods continue to exact a heavy toll in suffering and death, despite our considerable knowledge of the workings of the physical world. If science has offered only limited protection from the consequences of natural disasters, it has in no way diminished our fascination with them. Perhaps that's because the scale and power of natural disasters force us as individuals to confront our relatively insignificant place in the physical world and remind us of the fragility and transience of our lives. Perhaps it's because we can imagine ourselves in the midst of dire circumstances and wonder how we would respond. Perhaps it's because disasters seem to bring out the best and worst instincts of humanity: altruism and selfishness, courage and cowardice, generosity and greed.

As one of the national chairmen of the American Red Cross, a humanitarian organization that provides relief for victims of disasters, I have had the privilege of seeing some of humanity's best instincts. I have witnessed communities pulling together in the face of trauma; I have seen thousands of people answer the call to help total strangers in their time of need.

Of course, helping victims after a tragedy is not the only way, or even the best way, to deal with disaster. In many cases planning and preparation can minimize damage and loss of life—or even avoid a disaster entirely. For, as history repeatedly shows, many disasters are caused not by nature but by human folly, shortsightedness, and unethical conduct. For example, when a land developer wanted to create a lake for his exclusive resort club in Pennsylvania's Allegheny Mountains in 1880, he ignored expert warnings and cut corners in reconstructing an earthen dam. On May 31, 1889, the dam gave way, unleashing 20 million tons of water on the towns below. The Johnstown Flood, the deadliest in American history, claimed more than 2,200 lives. Greed and negligence would figure prominently in the Triangle Shirtwaist Company fire in 1911. Deplorable conditions in the garment sweatshop, along with a failure to give any thought to the safety of workers, led to the tragic deaths of 146 persons. Technology outstripped wisdom only a year later, when the designers of the luxury liner *Titanic* smugly declared their state-of-the-art ship "unsinkable," seeing no need to provide lifeboat capacity for everyone onboard. On the night of April 14, 1912, more than 1,500 passengers and crew paid for this hubris with their lives after the ship collided with an iceberg and sank. But human catastrophes aren't always the unforeseen consequences of carelessness or folly. In the 1940s the leaders of Nazi Germany purposefully and systematically set out to exterminate all Jews, along with Gypsies, homosexuals, the mentally ill, and other so-called undesirables. More recently terrorists have targeted random members of society, blowing up airplanes and buildings in an effort to advance their political agendas.

The books in the GREAT DISASTERS: REFORMS AND RAMIFICATIONS series examine these and other famous disasters, natural and human made. They explain the causes of the disasters, describe in detail how events unfolded, and paint vivid portraits of the people caught up in dangerous circumstances. But these books are more than just accounts of what happened to whom and why. For they place the disasters in historical perspective, showing how people's attitudes and actions changed and detailing the steps society took in the wake of each calamity. And in the end, the most important lesson we can learn from any disaster—as well as the most fitting tribute to those who suffered and died—is how to avoid a repeat in the future.

"In America,
They Don't
Let You Burn"

The gutted interior of the Triangle Shirtwaist Company's eighth-floor shop hints at the enormous human tragedy that occurred here on March 25, 1911.

The afternoon of Saturday, March 25, 1911, was much like any other in New York City. Classes were in session at New York University, located on the northeast end of Washington Square. Couples and families strolled through the park while shoppers walked along the streets, including Fifth Avenue, that led out of the square. Shopkeepers straightened their wares or swept their sidewalks as horse-drawn wagons made their way down the avenues.

Between 4:30 and 5:00 P.M., several hundred women and men were closing up shop on the top three floors of the 10-story Asch Building at the corner of Greene Street and Washington Place. The bells had just rung, signaling the end of a long workweek. Some employees were finishing up their work; others were receiving their wages or in cloakrooms gathering their belongings before heading home. On the ninth floor, coworkers passed around slices of cake to celebrate an employee's recent engagement. Others looked forward to enjoying themselves at a dance hall or theater that night.

Suddenly, people on Greene Street and in nearby shops heard what they described as a loud "puff" and the sound of breaking glass coming from the Asch Building. Then they saw a dark bundle fall from the eighth floor.

But it wasn't a bundle. It was a woman. Even as onlookers realized what it was, several more women had jumped from upper floors. Smoke poured out of the windows. The top of the Asch Building was on fire.

The eighth, ninth, and tenth floors of the Asch Building housed the Triangle Shirtwaist Company, a garment factory that employed between 200 and 800 people, depending on the season. Most of the Triangle employees were women, and some were recent immigrants who spoke only Yiddish or Italian. On March 25, 1911, about 500 workers were in the building. There might have been more, but some of Triangle's Jewish employees refused to work on the Sabbath, and the businesses on the other floors were already closed. If the fire had started just a few minutes later, nearly all of the workers would have already left.

The fire started on the eighth floor in one of the wooden-slatted bins that held fabric scraps. From there, the flames raced along, igniting the cutting tables and the floor. Men grabbed pails of water and tried to extinguish the flames, but within seconds the fire spread to fabric patterns hanging on a line above the

Firemen respond to the Triangle Shirtwaist fire in their horse-drawn wagon.

workers' heads. The patterns burned off the line and fell, igniting whatever they landed on.

A few pails of water could not stop the fire. There was too much that could burn, and burn quickly. Two workers, Samuel Bernstein and Louis Senderman, unraveled a fire hose that was stored in the stairwell. When they tried to turn on the water, nothing happened. Others grabbed the nozzle. Still, no water came out. The men turned their energies to helping others escape.

Within a minute or two, the flames spread across the eighth floor, out of the windows, and up to the ninth floor. Hundreds of people, mostly young women, pressed themselves against the doors and windows— anywhere to escape the heat, smoke, and flames. The two staircases in the building were so narrow that they allowed only one person at a time to go through them.

The staircases quickly became blocked by smoke and flames and by fainting and frantic people.

The only other escape routes, the freight elevators, were barred by heavy iron doors. Two passenger elevators, each with less than six square feet of floor space, were hand operated by cables that ran through the center of the cars. Although each elevator was supposed to hold a maximum of 15 people, operators Gaspar Mortillalo and Joseph Zito later said they each carried at least twice that number on the last trips they made.

One of the survivors, Irene Seivos, later remembered breaking the window of an elevator door with her hands and screaming that there was a fire. "It was so hot we could scarcely breathe," she said. "When the elevator did stop and the door opened at last, my dress was catching fire." The car quickly filled and just before the doors closed, Seivos leaped on top of other women who had jammed inside. Someone, she said, grabbed her hair from behind and tried to pull her out, but she kicked free.

One of the women Seivos landed on, Celia Saltz, recalled that when she first tried to open a staircase door, she found it locked. By then, "everybody was pushing and screaming" toward the passenger elevators. "I was pushed into [the car] by the crowd. I began to scream for my sister. I had lost, had lost my sister," Saltz remembered. Later, her 14-year-old sister, Minnie, found Celia outside, lying on the sidewalk and unconscious.

As bad as the situation was for the 225 workers on the eighth floor, conditions on the ninth floor were worse. Here, 350 workers had neither seen the fire start nor received an alarm by telephone, as the 60 workers on the 10th floor had. The ninth floor held 240 sewing machines on eight 75-foot tables, and flames raced along the oil-soaked wooden floors and wooden chairs, igniting the sewing machines, the wicker baskets holding flammable shirtwaists, and fabric scraps. Barrels of sewing-machine oil exploded.

On the ninth floor, frantic women found all the stairways and fire escape routes blocked, and they pressed against the elevator doors. Sarah Cammerstein watched an elevator descend and, certain that it would not come back, jumped and landed on the roof of the car, then blacked out. When she came to, she said, "I looked straight up the elevator shaft. I could see the flames coming out of the eighth floor. I couldn't move. But the elevator was moving. It was going up, straight to the flames. I began to scream. I found the strength to bang my fist on the top of the elevator." The car was lowered and Sarah was lifted to safety.

The elevator operators tried to make another trip. One elevator could not ascend to the eighth floor because the intense heat had bent its tracks. The other car could not rise at all. Workers on the ninth floor now pried open the elevator door, and the press of people pushed into the elevator shaft. Bodies fell on the roof of the car, nearly caving it in. Some workers, like Celia Walker, grabbed onto the cables suspending the elevator and attempted to lower themselves.

"I knew that in a few seconds I would be pushed into the shaft," Walker remembered. "I jumped for

The Asch Building's two passenger elevators, each with a capacity of about 15 persons, proved woefully inadequate in evacuating the hundreds of workers fleeing the fire. As this photo indicates, the rapidly spreading blaze soon rendered the elevators useless anyway.

Although the Asch Building had a small fire escape, it ended at the second floor, forcing workers to risk a frightening jump to the ground. But many people didn't even have that much of a chance: dozens plunged eight stories to their deaths when this section of the flimsy fire escape collapsed.

the center cable. I began to slide down. I remember passing the floor numbers up to five. Then something falling hit me." When Walker awoke in a hospital, she learned that she had been found on top of the elevator car at the bottom of the shaft. "Others had fallen on top of me. . . . Down the middle of my body I felt the burning of the cable which had torn right through my clothes," she said. While some had been pushed into the shaft, others had jumped and missed the cables. One woman, Sarah Friedman, fell into the shaft and passed out. When she awoke, she found herself lying in the street among the dead.

The Asch Building had one small fire escape, but

many Triangle employees did not even know it existed. The two windows leading to the escape had been locked and shuttered for months. The fire escape itself was a rickety, narrow structure—and it ended, for some reason, at the second floor. There, a drop ladder descended about 13 feet, forcing those who reached the bottom to jump the remaining six feet to the ground. Directly beneath the drop was the glass skylight over the basement. To make matters worse, the windows' huge, metal shutters, when opened, extended so far over the fire escape walkway that it was nearly impossible to get around them.

Ninth-floor workers tried to get to the fire escape. The women fought to unlock the window latches, then broke the windows and bashed at the shutters. At last they climbed out, racing to stay ahead of the searing heat. Soon the narrow metal fire escape became clogged with dozens of people. Under their weight, it began to bend. A group of women, including Rose Reiner, escaped the heaving, swaying fire escape when one of them smashed a sixth-floor window. The women re-entered the building only to find themselves trapped; the door to the staircase was locked. Policeman James Meehan, one of the first rescuers to arrive on the scene, was on his way up the stairs. Hearing the women's terrified cries, he forced open the door and released them.

Soon the entire fire escape, crammed with struggling people, separated from the building and dumped its passengers. Professor H. G. Parsons, in a neighboring building, heard the screams and ran to a window. "I was shocked by a sight more terrible than I ever could have imagined," he said. "I saw a fire escape literally gorged with girls. A great tongue of flame reached out for them." Bodies, some of them on fire, crashed through the basement skylight and others landed in the courtyard below. At the edge of the courtyard was a wall with an iron piling fence atop it. At least one woman's body was later found pierced through by the fence spikes.

All the while, other "bundles" were falling. Onlookers on the streets below watched, horrified, as flames shot from the upper-story windows and women, desperate to escape, jumped. Many were themselves on fire, and they left trails of smoke behind them as they plummeted to the sidewalk. Some observers shouted up to the terrified women, begging them not to jump; others ran to find blankets that they could use to catch those who did.

After what seemed an interminable wait but was only about three minutes, firefighters arrived in horse-drawn wagons and newly designed gas-powered trucks. New York City owned the finest fire fighting equipment of its day, and the newest high-water-pressure areas in the city included the block on which the Asch Building was located. But all the state-of-the-art technology was not enough. The water pressure was not strong enough for the spray to reach the upper-most floors of the building, and the firemen's ladders reached only to just below the seventh floor.

Some workers tried to jump onto the fire company ladders, but missed. On the street below, several strong men tried to catch jumpers using life nets. These were torn from rescuers' hands by the force of the falling bodies, which crashed to the sidewalk. Some people jumped two or three at a time, clinging to their friends for strength as they made the terrible decision: jump or burn. Eyewitnesses claim that few people jumped until their clothing was on fire and they had no choice. Firemen had to turn their hoses on the still-burning bodies on the sidewalk.

One woman who seemed to survive the horrifying leap was helped to her feet by Battalion Chief Edward Worth. "Now go right across the street," he instructed her. "She walked ten feet—and dropped. She died in one minute," he said.

Members of the crowd that had gathered on the streets watched several awful dramas unfold before their eyes. One woman, perched precariously on a ledge, removed her hat and tossed it into the air, then took out bills and coins from her handbag and flung them. Then she jumped. Another woman, Celia Weintraub, tried unsuccessfully to restrain her friend from jumping. Then Celia herself paused, stood up straight, and seemed to be speaking to the air before her. Finally, she too plunged downward. Weintraub lay under the wet, bloody corpses on the sidewalk for two hours until someone noticed that she was still alive. She died in a hospital a few days later.

Reporter William Shepherd, who happened to be walking on Greene Street when the fire began, telephoned his editor at the *New York World* and described what he saw as the fire raged. Published the next day, the newspaper account of the tragedy included a particularly heartbreaking scene:

A young man helped a girl to the window sill on the ninth floor. Then he held her out deliberately, away from the building, and let her drop. He held out a second girl the same way and let her drop. He held out a third girl who did not resist. I noticed that. They were all as unresisting as if he were helping them into a street car instead of into eternity. He saw that a terrible death awaited them in the flames and his was only a terrible chivalry. Then came the love amid the flames. He brought another girl to the window. I saw her put her arms around him and kiss him. Then he held her into space—and dropped her. Quick as a flash, he was on the window sill himself. His coat fluttered upwards—the air filled his trouser legs as he came down. I could see he wore tan shoes. . . . Later I saw his face. You could see he was a real man. He had done his best. We found later that in the room in which he stood, many girls were burning to death. He chose the easiest way and was brave enough to help the girl he loved to an easier death.

Some of the first workers to escape the fire, including Sylvia Reigler, were stopped by firemen as they tried to leave the building. "They were afraid we would be killed by the falling bodies," Sylvia explained later. But at the time, the frightened and confused workers thought that the firemen were preventing them from escaping the building. Reigler herself had just seen her friend catch fire and leap from a window. "I stood there screaming," she recalled, and soon afterwards was carried across the street to safety. Many of the dazed survivors went home immediately, trying to erase with normalcy the horror they had just experienced.

Before firemen ventured up the stairs of the Asch Building with their heavy hoses, Patrolman Meehan had already reached between the fifth and sixth floors

Crowds gathered in Washington Square and Greene Street to watch as the Triangle tragedy unfolded.

of the stairwell. There he was forced to press against the wall to allow a mass of struggling humans to pass. However, many more people remained trapped. On every floor, the doors to the stairs opened inward, and the press of desperate people trying to get out made it almost impossible to open the doors. With the flames behind them racing closer, the crowd couldn't move back from the door. The crush of bodies pressed harder as the air filled with thick black smoke.

On the ninth floor one such stairwell door had been locked, and several women passed out from the heat and smoke before they could find another way out. Fire blocked any escape behind them and the door would not give. These people, trapped on all sides, sought refuge from the conflagration behind a flimsy wooden barrier that enclosed the cloakroom. Firemen would later discover a pile of 13 bodies in this dressing room and find some door locks that still held. Behind one locked door they would find 20 more bodies.

Some workers on the ninth floor never even reached a stairwell or door. They were trapped at their sewing machines, blocked by the long tables. The narrow aisles were clogged with chairs, wicker baskets of completed work, fabric scraps, and other debris. Some women backed away from the flames toward the windows and were soon forced to jump. A few jumped across the tables from machine to machine. Others, too frightened or caught by the flames too quickly, did nothing at all. Ethel Monick, one of the workers on the ninth floor, looked up from her sewing machine and saw "fire coming in all around us. I saw women at other machines become frozen with fear. They never moved." New York City fire chief Edward Croker would later be sickened by the sight of several of these women, burned to bare bones, still sitting at their sewing machines.

Those agile and fortunate enough to hop across the tables often found exits blocked, locked, or clogged with people. Some people went up the stairs, rather than down, and though only one staircase reached the roof, that direction offered the best chance for survival. When ninth-floor Triangle employee Ida Nelson saw flames blocking the stairways, she quickly took a roll of fabric from a desk to use as a shield:

I wrapped it around and around me until only my face showed. Then I ran right into the fire on the stairway and up toward the roof. I couldn't breathe. The lawn [a light flammable fabric] caught fire. As I ran, I tried to keep peeling off the burning lawn, twisting and turning as I ran. By the time I passed the tenth floor and got to the roof, I had left most of the lawn in ashes behind me. But I still had one end of it under my arm. That was the arm that got burned.

When Ida got to the roof, another worker, Rose Cohen, helped her put out the flames on her clothing. Cohen herself, her hair smoldering, had narrowly

Authorities examine two of the dead. In the final moments of their lives, many workers faced an awful choice: flames and smoke or a fatal jump to the pavement.

escaped the ninth floor with one thought in her head: "All greenhorn immigrants like my parents used to say, 'In America, they don't let you burn.'"

Most of the 60 people working on the tenth floor, where Triangle's administrative offices were located, survived the blaze. New York University students and professors in a neighboring building saw the panic-stricken workers on the roof. The students rigged ladders, left behind by painters, so that survivors could crawl across them onto nearby roofs. The Asch Building roof was covered in smoke, and crawling across ladders suspended 10 stories above the ground was not easy—but it was better than jumping and certainly better than burning. Nearly everyone working on the 10th floor escaped, and some ninth-floor workers, including Ida Nelson and Rose Cohen, also escaped to neighboring roofs.

Perhaps the last person to escape was a young woman rescued by Charles Kramer, a university student helping survivors across the ladders. Kramer had climbed down to the Asch Building roof for one last check. By this time, the roof was completely engulfed in thick black smoke; it seemed deserted. Then Kramer heard moaning. He followed the sound and discovered the young woman near the stairway, unconscious, her hair smoldering. Kramer smothered the sparks and carried her to the ladder. To get her to safety, though, he had to wrap her hair around his hands and drag her.

The narrow staircases, the flimsy and ineffective fire escape, the crowded conditions and flammable materials that made escaping next to impossible, the lack of elevators—all of these conditions were, in 1911, perfectly legal. Joseph Asch, the owner of the building, had claimed it was fireproof—and it was. In the wake of the deadly fire, Asch declared:

> I have obeyed the law to the letter. There was not one detail of the construction of my building that was not submitted to the [New York] Building and Fire Departments. Every detail was approved and the Fire Marshal congratulated me. . . . I have never received any request or demand from any department or bureau for alteration to the building nor has any request or demand been received by me for additional fire escapes nor has the fire escape on the building ever been unfavorably criticized to me by any official.

"The architects," Asch said, "claimed that my building was ahead of any other building of its kind." He was right—his building was one of the few in the city that even had a fire escape. In 1911, no law required building sprinkler systems; no law regulated maximum occupancy of a building; and no law required fire drills, although they were recommended. Inspector Albert G. Ludwig, of the New York City Building Department noted that "this building could be worse and come within the requirements of the law." The Triangle Company, only one of the businesses in the building, had in almost all matters been in compliance with the law. The company premises had been inspected periodically and the firm was covered by fire insurance. Yet somehow, in just half an hour, 131 women and 15 men were dead.

Ninety Dimes a Week

2

T he Triangle Shirtwaist Company was part of the garment trade in New York City. As early as the 1850s and 1860s, the city's garment industry employed more than 100,000 workers in about 4,000 shops. Most of these shops were small and put out piecework. Pieceworkers worked in their homes and were paid not by the hour but by the number of finished pieces they produced. In the mid-1800s, the overwhelming majority of New York's garment workers were immigrants, mainly from Germany and Ireland. Especially after 1860, employers hired more women than men, because women were considered more submissive than men and companies could pay them less.

By the 1890s, many of the German and Irish immigrants of the previous generation of employees had worked their way up and owned their own companies. Part of the prosperity and success of these immigrants hinged on their desire to become "Americanized." They took pride in being culturally American, and most of them did not wish to associate socially with more recently arrived immigrants—"greenhorns" (newcomers) who still spoke with foreign accents. Nevertheless, many such garment factory owners preferred to hire workers with backgrounds similar to their own—in part out of a desire to Americanize them. As a result, Jewish immigrants to New York could rely on these German-born employers to provide employment.

In the 1890s, Jews emigrated by the thousands from Russia to escape the brutal pogroms (organized massacres) sweeping across the country. In that decade and the next, 90 percent of Russians who left their homeland immigrated to the United States; many of them stayed in New York City. A great number found jobs in the garment industry, and many preferred to work for Jewish employers.

These years also saw a great increase in the number of Italian immigrants. Max Blanck and Isaac Harris, the owners of the Triangle Shirtwaist Company, advertised extensively in Italian neighborhoods, believing that Italians made more docile workers.

In the late 1890s and early 1900s, not just the management but the garment industry itself changed. Clothing manufacturers began catering to women who preferred newer, more "liberal" styles of clothing. The published drawings of illustrator Charles Dana Gibson showed the ideal woman wearing a new style of long skirt and a blouse known as a "shirtwaist."

The shirtwaist was a tailored, long-sleeved, high-necked shirt that became "standard attire for thousands of young ladies taking positions with industrial and commercial enterprises." Although the shirt itself was a masculine garment, the softer fabric and the style of the shirtwaist was very feminine. One historian described the Gibson Girl, as she was called, as "a bright-eyed, fast-moving young lady, her long tresses knotted in a bun atop her proud head, ready to challenge the male in sport, drawing room, and, if properly equipped with paper cuff covers, even in the office." Shirtwaists became extremely popular, partly because they were ready-to-wear and relatively inexpensive.

As the demand for shirtwaists grew, so did the number of factories producing the garment.

By 1910, New York City alone had 450 shirtwaist factories. This number does not include the thousands of factories producing other garments, such as caps, coats, and dresses. Garment making was so important to the city that by 1910, nearly half of all New York City workers were employed in the industry. The city had more garment factories than anywhere else in the world.

Why did so many immigrant women find work in the garment industry? As the 20th century began, New York was a rapidly changing city. Immigrants, most of them European, arrived by the millions during the first

Every era has its ideal of beauty and style. For America in the early 1900s it was the Gibson Girl, a creation of illustrator Charles Dana Gibson. The distinctive long-sleeved blouse, called a shirtwaist, was an integral part of the Gibson Girl's look.

The typical garment sweatshop was cramped and cluttered, and women formed the majority of the work-force.

decade, and because most entered the United States through New York, they often settled permanently in the city. For Italian and Eastern European women in particular, who were often forced by economic necessity to work, the garment trades offered attractive jobs. Many immigrant women believed that working in a garment factory would enhance or improve the sewing skills they had learned in their homelands. This would enable them to sew clothing for themselves and their families, as well as sell it to others. Some of the profits could then go to relatives they had left behind in Europe.

What they did not know, however, was that jobs in the garment industry were so specialized that no one person completed a whole garment. A single shirtwaist might pass through as many as 30 pairs of hands before it was completed.

Consequently, when immigrant women did find garment jobs, the work was simple, repetitive, and boring. Moreover, it invariably paid poorly. In addition to the hundreds of thousands of employees in garment factories, many more took home piecework. This job was equally boring—making artificial flowers out of petals and stems, for example. Often children, some as young as three years old, were forced to help their mothers for 12 to 14 hours each day so that the completed work would bring enough money to pay for food. Despite the money earned, however, for many of these families breakfast was still a luxury.

New immigrants were impressed with the earnings they were able to take home from factory jobs—the wages often compared favorably to the earnings (if any) made in the "old country." But workers who had been in New York for some time realized that the costs of food and housing were much higher in the city than in their homeland. The meager New York wages hardly covered the bills. Even worse, if a family member became ill or for some other reason could not work, it was frighteningly easy to fall behind on paying bills, and there was virtually no way to catch up.

Among Italian immigrants in particular, men had work experience primarily in agricultural and menial labor. Any work they were able to find in the city was seasonal and low paid, so it was often left to the women, who had at least some sewing skills, to be the family breadwinners. Without their paychecks, the families would quite literally starve, or be put out on the street. Of all immigrants in New York City, Italian workers had the lowest average income and poorest standard of living.

For young single women, though, a factory job could provide some "pin money" (disposable income). With their wages, they could go to the dance hall or the theater, or buy a new hat occasionally if they skipped taking lunches and worked quickly. For these women, a job outside the home meant a new degree of freedom from otherwise strict parental supervision. If they managed to save a modest amount of money over the years—or if they chose their husbands well—some of these young women could quit their jobs when they married. Most, however, needed the income too badly and continued working whenever possible.

The intense competition for jobs in New York meant that another employee could always be hired to take a worker's place. Women workers in particular had to consider the fierce competition—they were never paid as much as men and were rarely if ever assigned a "skilled" position. They continually had to compete against better-paid men in the workplace.

Women workers also faced brazen harassment. Male employees teased, fondled, or even attacked women in some shops, often without reprimand or punishment. Some bosses required sexual favors in exchange for employment. Most working women did not encounter such offensive circumstances, but their situation was nonetheless different from that of their male coworkers.

Garment manufacturers themselves also faced stiff

competition. Between 1900 and 1910, new clothing companies sprang up almost overnight, particularly in New York. The clothing trade in general was seasonal, with only three or four busy months in the spring and two or three in the fall. With 450 shirtwaist factories in New York alone, few bosses of large factories were willing to let anything—even the safety of their shops—get in the way of profit making.

The shirtwaist trade was distinct from the other types of clothing trades: each shop produced a different style of shirtwaist in a different manner. Many of the largest shirtwaist companies, including Triangle, were located in the area around Fifth Avenue and

A mother and her children work assembling artificial flowers in their tenement, circa 1890. Because it could be done in the home, piecework—work for which a person received a set price per item completed—provided a vital source of income for immigrant families. Piecework was especially important in the garment industry.

Washington Square. What made the garment factories in this area distinct from others in New York was that all were located in buildings designed to be warehouses, not factories where hundreds of people worked.

In early 1911, reporters Sue Ainsley Clark and Edith Wyatt published a story supposedly told to them by a 16-year-old Russian Jewish worker named Natalya Perovskaya. (The story actually belonged to a 15-year-old girl named Rose Perr.) In it, "Natalya" described the difficult conditions under which she and many young immigrant women were forced to work:

> Mounting the stairs of the waist factory, one is aware of the heavy vibrations. The roar and whir of the machines increase as the door opens, and one sees in a long loft . . . rows and rows of girls with heads bent and eyes intent upon the flashing needles. They are all intensely absorbed; for if they be paid by the piece, they hurry from ambition, and if they be paid by the week, they are "speeded up" by the foreman to a pace set by the swiftest workers. . . . In the Broadway establishment, which may be called the Bruch Shirt-waist Factory, there were four hundred girls—six hundred in the busy season. The hours were long—from eight till half past twelve, a half hour for lunch, and then from one till half past six. Sometimes the girls worked until half past eight, until nine [P.M.]. There were only two elevators in the building, which contained other factories. There were two thousand working people to be accommodated by these elevators, all of whom began work at eight o'clock in the morning; so that, even if Natalya reached the foot of the shaft at half past seven, it was

sometimes half past eight before she reached the factory on the twelfth floor. She was docked for this tardiness so often that frequently she had only five dollars a week instead of six. This injustice, and the fact that sometimes the foreman kept them waiting needlessly for several hours before telling them that he had no work for them, was particularly wearing to the girls.

Rose Perr later became a labor leader, and told the following story to reporter Miriam Finn Scott:

My shop is a long and narrow loft on the fifth floor of the building, with the ceiling almost on our heads. In it one hundred electric-power machines are so closely packed together that, unless I am always on the lookout, my clothes or hair or hand is likely to catch in one of the whizzing machines. In the shop it is always night. The windows are only on the narrow ends of the room, so even the few girls who sit near them sew by gaslight most of the time, for the panes are so dirty the weak daylight hardly goes through them. The shop is swept only once a week; the air is so close that sometimes you can hardly breathe. . . . In the busy season . . . I put in what equals eight work-days in the week. Thirty minutes is allowed for lunch, which I must eat in the dressing-room four flights above the shop, on the ninth floor. These stairs I must always climb; the elevator, the boss says, is not for the shopgirls.

I began as a shirt-waist maker in this shop five years ago. For the first three weeks I got nothing, though I had already worked on a machine in Russia. Then the boss paid me three dollars a week. Now, after five years' experience, and I am considered a good worker, I am paid nine. But I never get the nine

Not all garment sweat-shops were large operations like the Triangle Shirtwaist Company. Many shops, such as the one shown here, employed only a handful of workers.

dollars. There are always 'charges' against me. If I laugh, or cry, or speak to a girl during work hours, I am fined ten cents for each 'crime.' Five cents is taken from my pay every week to pay for benzine [cleaning fluid] which is used to clean waists that have been soiled in the making; and even if I have not soiled a waist in a year, I must pay the five cents just the same. If I lose a little piece of lining, that possibly is worth two cents, I am charged ten cents for the goods and five cents for losing it. . . . Each of these things seems small, I know, but when you only earn ninety dimes a week, and are fined for this and fined for that, why, a lot of them are missing when pay day comes, and you know what it means when your money is the only reg-ular money that comes in a family of eight.

Aside from horribly unsanitary working conditions, many workers suffered the whims of their bosses, who were not above "dirty tricks" to get more work out of them. One young girl explained in 1909 that her supervisor, employed by the Bijou Waist Company, "[moved] the hands of the clock when we did not see it. Sometimes we found that we got 20 minutes for lunch and that when the clock showed five it was really after six." Another young woman remarked that her boss gave his workers tiny slips of paper on which to record their work and hand in before they would be paid. "The boss has these slips made small purposely, so they'll be easier to lose," she said. "One week I lost two of these tiny pieces of paper, and I could not get one cent for the work I had done. It was half my week's wages. Every day some of us lose these tickets."

Garment workers were also subject to regular layoffs when business was slow. Employees could be out of work for four to eight weeks at a time several times a year—a very serious situation for people who needed every cent they could earn. But factory owners could always find someone else who was willing to take the job. Often, too, employers hired "learners"—new, inexperienced workers who would take a lower pay rate than the "old hands." Sometimes learners earned nothing at all until they proved that they were "experienced enough." This employment method was quite popular: during the period that the shirtwaist was in vogue, up to a quarter of all garment workers in New York—about 200,000 people—were learners.

The average yearly wage for women in this industry, taking into account the slack seasons when no work was available, was about five dollars a week, or

$250 a year. More experienced workers averaged about seven or eight dollars a week (about $350 to $400 a year). If it is true, as one historian notes, that a working family of five needed to make $1,000 each year "in order to survive at even a subsistence level," then garment workers must have fought a constant battle to survive well below poverty level.

And out of these meager wages, as Rose Perr noted, workers were fined for the most minor infractions and mistakes. If a worker arrived late in the morning, for example, she might be fined one cent for each minute of the time she missed, even if she only earned about 15 cents in an hour. Or she might be prevented from working until after lunch, thereby forfeiting half a day's wages for only a few minutes' tardiness. Employers even deducted from their workers' pay the cost of the needles and thread they used.

Not surprisingly, few employers paid extra wages for overtime work. An ordinary workweek was 55 to 60 hours long. Particularly during the busy seasons, employers expected workers to stay late each night and to come to work seven days a week—without additional compensation. If they did not, they were let go. "If you don't come in on Sunday, don't come in on Monday," read a sign at the Triangle Shirtwaist Company during one busy season.

Garment workers were not completely at the mercy of their employers. An 1899 New York state law forbade women and minors to work more than 10 hours a day or 60 hours a week. There was some question whether such laws interfered with businessmen's rights, but after the U.S. Supreme Court decided in 1908 that such laws were valid, more states limited work hours for women and children. In 1912, the New York state legislature revised its earlier law, limiting all females and males under age 18 to only nine hours a day or 54 hours a week.

But these laws were not always carefully enforced. Because of the seasonal nature of the garment industry, employees were often willing to work longer whenever they had the opportunity. And if garment workers were annoyed by their employers' breaking these laws, how could they dare to complain when they needed the money so badly?

After a state law was passed in 1890 that discouraged the practice of hiring on a piecework basis, garment work increasingly became centered in factories. But manufacturers also hired "subcontractors"— workers (nearly always male) employed by the manufacturer and given a set amount of work to complete. Subcontractors would then either hire homeworkers or, after the 1890s, hire their own employees to fulfill the work contract out of their own shops or at the manufacturer's shop.

Employees hired in this way had no contact with the business's actual owner, only with their immediate supervisor, the subcontractor. And these employees were not listed on the original employer's payroll; only the subcontractor, referred to as a "team leader," was considered to be officially employed by the firm. As a result, companies like Triangle that worked with subcontractors had no accurate records of how many workers were present in their factories on any given day.

"They're a Lot of Cattle Anyway"

When the Industrial Revolution swept through America in the latter half of the 19th century, few laws existed to regulate child labor, and children as young as five or six formed an important—if scandalously exploited—part of the workforce.

3

In November 1910, the Wolf Muslin Undergarment Company in Newark, New Jersey, caught fire. At least one insurance company had classified the building that housed the factory as an "extra-hazard" because it was not fireproof. Twenty-five women perished in the fire; most of them died after jumping out of fourth-story windows onto the street below. Neither the company nor the building owner was punished or even held accountable for the women's deaths. Nor were the Newark city labor or building inspectors blamed. New York City fire chief Edward Croker warned the city that a similar tragedy could happen there at any time. He publicly urged that city officials under-take a plan to improve preparedness for emergencies in New York's

Exterior of the Asch Building. Note the Triangle Company sign on the eighth floor.

factories. Within six months, his prediction came to pass at the Triangle Shirtwaist Company.

Just days after the Triangle fire, the Women's Trade Union League (WTUL) held an inquiry, inviting New York factory workers to lodge anonymous complaints about their working conditions. The report provides a clear and disturbing portrait of the hazards that garment workers faced every day. According to workers from other factories, the dangerous conditions at Triangle had not been unusual; workers complained to the WTUL about dark, narrow staircases and hallways that were often obstructed. They also complained about poor ventilation, noting that what windows they had access to were frequently closed and almost always locked. And, workers noted, although most factory buildings were fairly high—some, like Triangle, as high as 10 stories—they never had enough elevators or staircases for their capacity. Most of these buildings had no fire escapes either, and many of the workers who complained to the WTUL mentioned that doors were often locked, or they opened inward.

It was reported that the machines and materials used in garment factories were equally hazardous. The sewing machines, pressing machines, steam tables, buttonhole machines, and the motors that drove them were not enclosed and did not have safety guards. Workers commonly caught their clothing, hair, or fingers in moving parts. And the noise and vibrations of the machinery in many shops was nearly unbearable: one had to shout to be heard, even if the listener was at one's side. At Triangle and some other shops, however, talking and singing were prohibited anyway, though supervisors frequently shouted at workers to move faster.

The fabrics with which employees worked were usually flammable, and the fabric scraps from completed projects lay around in huge piles. Lubricating oil, cleaning solutions, alcohol, and other combustible chemicals were regularly used but not always handled safely. Even worse, although smoking was prohibited in factories, some male employees ignored the rule and then tossed their matches or cigarette butts onto the floors.

Many workers also reported that even their most basic hygiene needs were ignored: some factories provided only one or two toilets for hundreds of workers, and even those scant facilities rarely functioned properly. Many shops had no sinks or washbasins; some had no running water at all. In general, the workers complained, the shops in which they worked were foul-smelling and dangerously filthy.

The employees who reported safety violations to the WTUL knew that complaining to their employers would have no effect on their working conditions— and it might even destroy their ability to hold a job. It was common knowledge at Triangle, for example, that complainers were automatically "blacklisted." In other words, their names were added to a list of known "troublemakers," and the list was shared with other factory employers in an attempt to lock those workers out of jobs. Without union protection, employees could do little to improve conditions.

A study of 1,243 shops in New York City, conducted by the New York Joint Board of Sanitary Control a few months before the Triangle fire, had yielded similarly appalling findings. The board's report, which was published in a magazine only nine days before the Triangle fire, noted the following hazardous conditions:

> Ninety-nine per cent of the shops were found to be defective in respect to safety: 14 had no fire escapes; 101 had defective drop ladders; 491 had only one exit; 23 had locked doors during the day; 58 had dark hallways; 78 had obstructed approaches to fire escapes; and 1,172, or 94 per cent, had doors opening in instead of out. Only one [shop] had ever had a fire drill.

These numbers are even more shocking when one considers that the report covered only the 1,243 factories that board members were able to inspect. At the time, New York City contained about 30,000 garment factories with 612,000 workers. In 1911, the WTUL reported that about half of those workers were employed in shops situated on or above the seventh floors of buildings, where standard fire ladders and hoses could not reach. Thousands more factories had been established in nearby Newark, New Jersey, as well as in other U.S. cities. And at the time, New York's labor and building regulations were considered the most progressive and advanced in the nation.

Conditions in loft buildings—those that were

intended to be used as warehouses—were particularly crowded, no matter how big the room was. As many as 500 workers might be crammed onto one floor of a shop. Every inch of space was filled with whirring machines, harried workers, raw materials, and finished pieces.

The law required that each worker have 250 cubic feet of air space (rather than floor space). Because the ceilings were unusually high in loft buildings, employers had great leeway to pack in workers and equipment. Each worker may have been allotted 250 cubic feet of air space, but most of it was above her head, not on the floor—where she most needed it.

Because most staircases in factory buildings were extremely narrow and allowed only one person at a time to ascend (or descend), a worker might spend a full hour getting from the ground floor to the factory floor. Employees in buildings with elevators were not much better off: garment worker "Natalya Perovskaya" (Rose Perr) reported that only two elevators accommodated the more than 2,000 workers in her building.

Constructed in 1901, the Asch Building had two staircases, although the square footage of its floors was such that three staircases should have been incorporated. The building's architect had claimed that a fire escape counted for the third staircase. When a building inspector noted that the fire escape ended above a glass basement skylight, the architect countered that the

IF YOU DON'T COME IN SUNDAY DON'T COME IN MONDAY.

THE MANAGEMENT

A notice posted at a garment sweatshop lets employees know that they must work Sundays. Before the rise of labor unions, management had almost unlimited power to set working conditions. Workers who complained, in addition to getting fired, often found themselves blacklisted by other employers.

escape would also lead to the back alley of the building. By the time of the fire, however, neighboring buildings had been erected and modified so that the Asch Building's fire escape ended not only over the skylight but also in an enclosed courtyard. There was no way out of the courtyard except through the building itself. Yet the Asch Building was considered safe because it had a fire escape when most similar buildings did not.

It is difficult to imagine what the scope of the tragedy at Triangle might have been had the Asch Building stairways not been separated from the interior of the building and constructed of slate and metal—noncombustible materials. Other buildings had wooden stairwells, or their staircases were lodged in air shafts. If a similar fire had broken out in one of those buildings, the staircases would have become like chimneys—feeding the fire, allowing it to spread more rapidly, and preventing escape.

Although the building inspector recommended changes to the Asch Building's architect, he had no way to require that the changes be made. Leon Stein, the author of the 1962 book *The Triangle Fire*, notes that only 47 building inspectors were responsible for 50,000 buildings in Manhattan alone. The city's fire department had categorized more than 13,000 buildings as too dangerous, but in February 1911, building department inspectors had been able to visit only about 2,000 of them. There simply were not enough inspectors.

Because of the shortage of inspectors, factory owners and bosses could predict—or pay bribes to be warned— when inspectors were due to arrive. Moreover, inspectors commonly contacted a shop authority before touring the location; as a result, owners and managers had time to quickly—and usually temporarily—fix some of the more serious violations. One especially common violation was the employment of children.

Shortly after the Triangle Shirtwaist Company moved into the Asch Building in 1902, Pauline Newman began her job there. She was still a child and thus was not legally employable; nevertheless, she worked from 7:30 A.M. to as late as 9:00 P.M. during Triangle's busy season, doing nothing but cutting threads off completed shirtwaists. She was paid $1.50 a week, whether she worked overtime or not. Triangle's owners, Max Blanck and Isaac Harris, were alerted whenever inspectors were due to arrive. The factory owners avoided citations for employing children by ordering Pauline and all other child workers to climb into the big storage bins that held completed shirtwaists. Other employees would then cover up the children, who remained hidden until the inspectors left the premises.

Violations of child-labor laws were not the only problems factory owners routinely covered up, but it was widely known that inspectors could be bribed to ignore violations or that the violations could easily be temporarily fixed for inspection. Critics claimed, with some truth, that New York City's building and labor inspectors were easily corrupted or else not qualified to judge the safety of buildings. But even qualified, honest inspectors had no efficient way of enforcing building and labor regulations.

The regulations themselves were sometimes so vague as to be useless. For example, one labor code in New York City required that doors to staircases open outwardly "where practicable." In the Asch Building, the stairs were so narrow that if the doors had been made to open outward, they would have knocked anyone on the top few steps down the stairs. Using outward-opening doors was not "practicable," so all the doors in the Asch Building opened inward.

City officials who argued for more stringent building laws were shot down by powerful groups of manufacturers. These groups claimed the government had no right to interfere in the marketplace or to "penalize" the captains of industry with "unnecessary" building costs. The political mood of America at the time was pro-business, and laws making employers liable for accidents in the workplace were widely thought to interfere with a citizen's (the employer's) constitutional right to use his property as he saw fit. As a result, no such laws were passed. Those who did demand stricter safety rules lost many legal and political battles.

In the garment industry, the workplace was full of fire hazards. At Triangle, the thousands of pounds of fabric and finished shirtwaists sat alongside barrels of flammable sewing machine oil on the eighth and ninth floors. Underneath the 240 sewing machines, floors were soaked through with the oil. Forty "cutters" (workers who cut the fabric into pieces) were employed at Triangle, and beneath each cutter's table stood a huge bin to hold fabric scraps. Triangle sold its scraps to a rag collector named Louis Levy, who came around every few months. The last time that Levy made a pickup was January, 1911, when he collected about three months' worth of accumulated rags. "They came from the eighth floor," he said later. "Altogether, it was 2,252 pounds." It is likely that there was a similar amount of flammable scraps at Triangle when the blaze broke out. The type of fabric used in shirtwaists

was more combustible than paper.

The physical arrangement of machinery and equipment at Triangle did not allow employees to have easy access or exit. On the ninth floor each of the tables that held the sewing machines was 75 feet long, with no aisles or breaks that would allow workers to pass through. A woman stationed at a machine in the middle of a table or close to a window would find it next to impossible to get out quickly.

In October 1910, the fire department had sent an official to the Asch Building for a routine inspection. The inspector's report noted that 259 water pails were stationed throughout the 10-story building, and a

This cellar skylight was broken by the bodies of Triangle workers who jumped several stories to escape the flames.

Unlike this factory, which was constructed almost entirely of wood, the Triangle shop was housed in a steel and stone building with safety features such as a fire escape and stairwells made of noncombustible materials. By the standards of the day, Triangle was deemed safe.

5,000-gallon water tank was located on the roof. In addition, each floor had a standpipe hose that could be connected to the roof tank in case of an emergency. The man responsible for inspecting the condition of the hose later admitted, however, that he "never did more than glance at it and never realized that [it] had rotted and disintegrated in the folds."

The owners of the Triangle Shirtwaist Company were not totally oblivious to the possibility of a fire in the building. But few manufacturers in New York at the time were interested in protecting their workers. One factory owner, when approached by an expert who offered to arrange fire drills for the employees at his company, declared, "Let 'em burn up. They're a lot of cattle anyway."

Perhaps most reprehensible was the fact that while Blanck and Harris neglected to provide a safe working environment for their employees, they nevertheless repeatedly increased the amount of fire insurance they held in the months before the fire.

Triangle was known in the insurance business as a "rotten risk," or a "repeater," meaning that the company collected insurance money fairly regularly for fires on its premises. There had already been several fires on company premises. Twice in 1902, once in 1904, and five times between 1905 and 1910, Harris and Blanck had collected insurance money for fires that occurred either in the Triangle Company or in another jointly owned business, the Diamond Company. Most of these fires had broken out after business hours, so no one had been injured. The fires were considered suspicious, however.

At the time of the 1911 fire, the Triangle Company was actually overinsured by about $80,000. This means that the amount of insurance the owners carried was higher than the actual worth of the company, its materials, and its equipment combined. The fire on March 25, 1911, was undoubtedly an unintended tragedy, but because Harris and Blanck were so heavily insured, they actually made a *profit* when their company was destroyed by fire.

Some employees, who had deplored the conditions at Triangle and believed the worst of its owners, were convinced that the fire had been deliberately set. This is extremely unlikely; for one thing, both Max Blanck and Isaac Harris had relatives working at Triangle that day. Also, Max Blanck's two young daughters were in the 10th-floor office waiting for their father when the fire broke out, and both he and his children were themselves lucky to have escaped.

During the early 1900s, the shirtwaist industry had undergone several upheavals. A recession in 1903 and a financial panic in 1907 had destabilized American businesses, and many factory owners had suffered further financial setbacks from periodic strikes and other labor problems. At the same time, new shirtwaist companies kept springing up, intensifying the competition. Many owners firmly believed that the only way they could profit in the shirtwaist business was to severely reduce the costs of production. Most often this was achieved by hiring fewer workers, making them work harder, and paying them as little as possible.

In this highly competitive business atmosphere, factory owners increasingly turned to subcontractors, who would hire their own workers to complete a job for the company. Subcontractors usually kept back some of the money they received before paying their own workers. Thus, subcontracted employees had no idea what the company was actually paying for the work they did. As a result, those who became frustrated and angry over the low pay they received took out their rage on the contractor, not on the owner.

Not all contractors were slave drivers, however. Many of them hired their own relatives and friends, and they tried to be as fair as possible to all of their employees. Some even got into trouble with their bosses when they attempted to get a better deal for their "girls." At Triangle, three systems of employment were used: some workers were paid a weekly salary; others were paid by the piece; still others worked under a subcontractor in "teams" on the site. It was one of the male subcontractors for Blanck and Harris who could be credited with sparking the strike at Triangle in 1909.

The Uprising of the Twenty Thousand

After hours in a garment sweatshop. Note the boxes of fabric, the scraps on the floor, and the extremely confined conditions between the two rows of sewing tables at right. Conditions such as these combined to make the Triangle fire so deadly.

4

O n November 22, 1909, about 16 months before the Triangle Company fire, a large meeting of garment workers convened in New York City and voted to go on a general (industry-wide) strike. It was a valiant decision: the workers who attended the meeting had no idea how many other workers in each of their shops had taken the oath to strike, or how many would actually go on strike. Each feared that when the time came, he or she might be the only one to do so.

The next morning the prospective strikers went to their workplaces as usual. Natalya Urisova, who was present at the previous day's meeting, recalled the atmosphere at the factory where she worked:

Women in favor of unionization march through Washington Square in New York City.

We all sat at the machines with our hats and coats beside us, ready to leave. The foreman had no work for us when we got there. But, just as always, he did not tell when there would be any, or if there would be any at all that day. And there was whispering and talking softly all around the room among the machines: "Shall we wait like this?" "There is a general strike." "Who will get up first?" "It would be better to be the last to get up, and then the company might remember it of you afterward, and do well for you." But I told them, "What difference does it make which one is first and which one is last?" Well, so we stayed whispering . . . not making up our minds, for two hours.

Then I started to get up. And at just the same minute all—we all got up together, in one second. No one after the other; no one before. And when I saw it—that time—oh, it excites me so yet, I can hardly talk about it. . . . [We] all walked out together. And already out on the sidewalk in front the policemen stood with the clubs. One of them said, "If you don't behave, you'll get this on your head." And he shook his club at me.

We hardly knew where to go—what to do next. But one of the American girls, who knew how to telephone, called up the Women's Trade Union League, and they told us all to come to a big hall a few blocks away. Then a leader spoke to us and told us about picketing quietly, and the law.

Thus began the strike that became known as "The Uprising of the Twenty Thousand," although many more would participate. For the first time in U.S. history, most of the striking workers were women.

Garment workers in New York City had been moving toward a general strike for some time. Managers, if not the owners of companies themselves, were not above resorting to rough handling of their employees to maintain order and avoid addressing complaints. In 1908, the year before the Uprising, the Triangle Company had pushed at least one employee too far. Subcontractors Jake Kline and Morris Elzufin had approached their supervisor to protest the meager wages remaining for them after they paid their "girls." The supervisor told them to finish their work and leave.

While the men were finishing, a "toughie," one of the manager's hirelings, came up to the men at their machines, broke the threads, and ordered them to leave immediately. Kline refused, saying that he had to finish his work or he would forfeit his wages. Kline and Elzufin were then physically removed from the shop. "With his shirt torn and his glasses broken," historian Leon Stein relates in *The Triangle Fire*, "Jake managed to twist free for a moment and shouted into the shop, where all work had stopped: 'People . . . workers . . . look what they are doing to us. . . . Get up from your machines!'"

They did; several hundred workers walked out of Triangle that day. Some went to the local chapter of the International Ladies Garment Workers' Union (ILGWU) to ask the union's help in launching a strike. But they were disappointed; the three-year-old chapter, Local 25, had little to offer them. With about 100 members and funds totaling just four dollars, the ILGWU chapter advised the workers to return to Triangle and make peace with the manager.

After the walkout, Triangle's managers began their own company union, but the group was exclusive. Many members were relatives and friends of the owners, and this fostered resentment among nonmembers. After a time, even the company union members grew discouraged and disgusted. In September 1909, seven members of the company union were absent from a meeting, and they were reported to management. When the union members arrived for work the next morning, they were locked out.

The fledgling local union could not ignore a lockout. So on September 27, Local 25 declared a strike at Triangle. Some workers at another shirtwaist manufacturer, the Leiserson Company, had been on strike

since July. Triangle employees were urged to join the Leiserson workers in protest of their mistreatment.

As news of the strike spread to other shirtwaist makers, more and more workers joined the protest. Nearly everyone in the garment trades had something to gain if the strike succeeded. Thousands of workers signed up with the ILGWU as union members.

The ILGWU and WTUL provided several needed services on behalf of their members. In theory, a union helped workers achieve better working conditions, and in practice, this involved a variety of tasks. The union had to enroll new members; negotiate contracts with

Samuel Gompers, head of the American Federation of Labor, addresses workers at a meeting called by the International Ladies Garment Workers Union, November 22, 1909. After the meeting, 40,000 workers participated in a general strike against hundreds of shirtwaist makers.

employers who wished to settle strikes; organize picketers and ensure they knew the rules of picketing; and raise money to bail out jailed strikers and support their families. To draw public attention to the workers' demands, the union also arranged newspaper and magazine coverage. Because the strike at Triangle began spontaneously, the ILGWU was unprepared and found itself struggling to achieve its goals "virtually overnight."

What exactly did the striking workers want? Their demands, although they sound perfectly reasonable to us today, were radical for the time. They wanted a 54-hour workweek. They wanted to be paid for working overtime. They wanted to abolish the subcontractor system and do away with the fines for "infractions" that unfairly depleted their pay. They wanted safer workplaces. Most important, the workers demanded that employers recognize their union's right to negotiate for them. Should another dispute arise, the workers wanted someone who would officially represent them before their seemingly all-powerful bosses. Strikes hurt the workers too—they lost much-needed income. A union would help resolve disputes before striking became necessary.

In early November 1909, *Survey* magazine reported on the situation at a picket line: "The Triangle Waist Company girls have been entirely orderly, but . . . the [police] officers break in upon any who are talking together; men loafing about in the employ of the company have insulted the girls; and the least resistance or answering back by the women is made excuse for a prompt arrest." More than 700 strikers were arrested for picketing; afterwards, many of the women were scolded and fined by judges, who would not even listen to their side of the story.

Until November 4, the strikers received little public attention and little sympathy from newspapers not already concerned with labor issues. On that day, however, the president of the New York chapter of the WTUL, Mary Dreier, was arrested while picketing. Witnesses paid by Triangle claimed that she had threatened a strikebreaker, but the judge, visibly embarrassed by Dreier's presence in his courtroom, dismissed the charge and released her.

The arrests of poor immigrant women may not have been news, but the arrest of a prominent, middle-class woman certainly was. This event and others like it, covered by major newspapers such as the *New York Times*, aroused a great deal of public sympathy and support for the strikers.

A few weeks later, on November 22, the ILGWU called a mass meeting at Cooper Union in New York City. So many thousands of workers showed up that "overflow" meetings were held in several other large venues. Participating speakers included Samuel Gompers, president of the American Federation of Labor (a coalition of labor unions) and Mary Dreier, as well as several others who debated the wisdom of the strike and its prospects for success. But when Clara Lemlich, a young shirtwaist maker and executive member of Local 25, spoke, her words transfixed the audience.

A petite young woman, who had already been beaten and arrested for picketing the Leiserson Company, Clara addressed the crowd in Yiddish. "I have listened to all the speakers, and I have no further patience for talk," she said. She called for a general strike. The workers cheered, and all present took an ancient Hebrew oath to keep faith. During the following week, as many as 40,000 shirtwaist workers went on strike at hundreds of shops in the area.

It should be remembered that many of the shirtwaist workers affected by the strike were under age 20, and that women did not yet have the right to vote. The expectation of women being docile and submissive was one reason why factories hired so many women: they were supposedly less likely to cause trouble.

But many of the strikers had been working for years under harsh conditions they described to anyone who would listen. In addition to sexism, many of them faced widely held prejudices against foreigners, particularly against groups such as Russians and Jews. Despite their youth and seemingly "frail" appearance, as described in many newspaper accounts, the female strikers were credited with having "held out" for their demands much longer than their male counterparts would have. Author Susan Glenn quotes one observer of the strike as insisting, "If any shops did go to work without settlement, it was because a majority in that shop were men."

Many shirtwaist companies were so small that they could not afford a lengthy strike. Within a week or two after the strike announcement, most of these companies agreed to the workers' demands. But the larger companies, including Triangle, refused to concede to the strikers. For them, the major stumbling block to an agreement was union recognition: they viewed union negotiators as "outsiders" who would tell them how to run their businesses.

The workers who continued to strike believed that

Garment workers congregate outside a polling place after voting on whether or not to strike.

it was time they organized and confronted their powerful employers. But Triangle and other companies fought back. They refused to discuss the union's demands, and they hired strikebreakers ("scabs") who agreed to work for them despite the strike. One large company set up cots in its factory to keep the strikebreakers from leaving and joining picketers outside. Other companies hired thugs and bribed policemen to beat up or arrest the strikers, despite the fact that most of them had followed the rules for peaceful picketing and broken no laws. And in November, Triangle owner Max Blanck even claimed against all evidence that there

Rose Schneiderman, one of the leaders of the Uprising of the Twenty Thousand, poses with a union banner.

was no strike, that the majority of Triangle's employees, or at least the American and Irish workers, were "loyal" and contented. This implied that the strike had been sparked by just a few troublemakers—by which he meant foreigners—who opposed Triangle's policies.

Max Blanck and Isaac Harris went even further. They urged their competitors to join them in their own "union," the Employers' Mutual Protective Association, later called the Waist and Dressmakers Manufacturers' Association. Arguing that the strikers interfered with the company owners' rights as businessmen by disrupting commerce, the shirtwaist manufacturers joined forces to defeat the union and the strikers.

Meanwhile, the strikers kept picketing, singing rallying songs in Yiddish and Italian. Fights and arrests continued. Workers participated in organized marches and attended rallies coordinated by labor unions. Within a few months, workers began achieving some surprising victories, in part because of the attention given not only from the press but also from social reformers and philanthropists.

On December 3, 1909, several thousand strikers, led by Mary Dreier, marched to City Hall, where they sought to present the mayor with a petition signed by about 30,000 shirtwaist makers. The petition described the unjust manner in which the strikers had been treated by police; indeed, the marchers had been stopped near City Hall that day by a contingent of mounted officers. The newspaper reports of this march gained the strikers much public sympathy and even monetary donations.

Less than two weeks later, Mary Dreier, Rose Schneiderman, and other female strike leaders met with wealthy supporters at an exclusive Manhattan club. Socialite Mrs. O. H. P. Belmont and Anne Morgan, daughter of banker J. P. Morgan, and others donated more than $1,300 to the cause that day. More valuable than the money, however, was the image of poor immigrant working women meeting and winning over the wealthiest of the world's upper classes. The meeting made a tremendous impression on the public. So too did the fact that these wealthy women also posted bail for strikers who had been arrested.

A special edition of the *Call* newspaper was printed on December 29, 1909. Small armies of women strikers fanned out to sell copies, with the proceeds benefiting the strikers' fund. On January 6, 1910, the *New York Journal* followed suit. In the weeks following the publication of the special newspaper editions, students attending Vassar, Wellesley, Smith, and other women's colleges also extended financial support and joined the picketers.

Workers in other cities also supported the striking shirtwaist workers. In Philadelphia, shirtwaist workers refused to complete jobs contracted by striking New York firms and went on strike themselves on December 20, 1909. Similar situations in Newark, New Jersey, and Hartford, Connecticut, meant that the large New

York shirtwaist manufacturers had even greater difficulty turning out their products. As a result, the Manufacturers' Association finally offered to meet all union demands except that of the "closed shop." In a closed shop, employers hire only union workers. An open shop employs both union and nonunion workers. A union shop, by contrast, allows employers to hire anyone, but new workers must join the union within a set period of time.

Strikers voted to reject the association's offer. The manufacturers refused to consider union recognition. Faced with this impasse, the months-long strike began losing momentum. Many strikers had returned to work in the more than 300 shops that had settled. By February 1, 1910, says one source, "the [shirtwaist] trade was operating at almost full production."

Some of the largest companies, like Triangle, refused to consider any strikers' demands. The Leiserson Company, after holding out for more than six months, finally settled on January 22, 1910, and three other members of the Manufacturers' Association settled around the same time. But 13 companies did not settle; between 1,000 and 6,000 workers were still on strike when, on February 15, the ILGWU declared the strike officially over.

The Uprising of the Twenty Thousand may have ended undramatically, but shirtwaist workers had made important gains. Most shops accepted the demand for a 54-hour workweek and did away with the subcontractor system; many agreed to compensate employees for overtime and to limit obligatory overtime. And workers would no longer have to pay for the needles and thread they used. Generally, wages were increased, but because

each shop set its own pay scales, the exact amount of the increases was impossible to calculate.

Perhaps most important, the strike had captivated the public and demanded that it pay attention to the harsh and dangerous conditions millions of factory workers faced daily. The trials of the strikers who were arrested, beaten, and thrown in jail for picketing turned public opinion in favor of laborers and against factory owners and managers. In addition, a committee known as the New York Joint Board of Sanitary Control was

Shirtwaist makers march toward City Hall to petition New York's mayor for protection. Though the workers were well within their rights to strike, they faced physical intimidation from thugs hired by their employers—and sometimes from police.

created to investigate working conditions in several thousand New York factories.

However, in the year following the strike, a number of shirtwaist manufacturers either moved out of the New York area or went out of business. Moreover, settlements made by individual companies allowed for no standardization of conditions. The only recourse many workers had was to go on strike once more. They would do so in the winter of 1910-11, after employers locked their workers out during a seasonal lull rather than renew union contracts.

Even though Triangle owners Harris and Blanck "won" the 1909–10 strike, they became even more circumspect about whom they hired. Each potential worker was carefully questioned—even investigated—about his or her attitude toward labor unions. The author of a 1996 study on the Triangle fire notes that even those already employed at Triangle were "questioned from time to time about [their] union sympathies and discharged if [their] answers did not meet with the approval of the company."

Nevertheless, the Uprising of the Twenty Thousand, the first major strike by women in the United States, set an important precedent. In 1910 and 1911, other garment workers also struck, not only in New York but also in other cities. New unions, such as the Amalgamated Clothing Workers of America (ACW) and the United Garment Workers (UGW), formed during the 1910s. Two-thirds of ILGWU members and one-third of ACW members were women. In the 1910s and 1920s, the ILGWU and other labor organizations would enroll hundreds of thousands of garment workers in unions, and women, especially Jewish women, would be major participants. In her 1990 book *Daughters of the Shtetl: Life and Labor in the Immigrant Generation*, author Susan Glenn reports that "nowhere else in the industrial landscape did women workers display the same commitment to labor organization."

Although the unions undoubtedly helped male factory employees achieve better working conditions as well, the garment industry, like other trades such as textiles, tobacco, and telephone/telegraph, relied heavily on women workers. It is not difficult to understand why many historians hail the Uprising of the Twenty Thousand as the beginning of the women's labor movement in America.

Despite the successes gained by striking garment workers, warning signs of impending disasters in New York's factories were apparent. Even after the public became aware of the industry's appalling working conditions, many factories did not remedy the situation, and preparedness for emergencies was practically nonexistent. It would take a large-scale tragedy involving nearly 150 deaths to bring about widespread change.

LOFTS
TO LET
F & G. PFLOMM
9 W. 29 ST

FOR SALE
42 X 96
F & G. PFLOMM
9 W. 29 ST

WAIST

MEYERS
CROWN
&
WALLACH

CLOTHING

PLUM

CLOTHING

HARRIS
BROS
MEN'S
CLOTHING

CLOAKS
SUITS

Firemen battle the Triangle blaze. Though the Asch Building was located within one of New York City's new high-water-pressure areas, the fire-fighting equipment of the day was otherwise inadequate for dealing with blazes in tall buildings.

The Reckoning

Although New York firemen had the Triangle blaze under control in less than 20 minutes, they continued spraying water to ensure the fire went out. Other rescuers faced a more gruesome task. The water running from the building into the gutters was red with the blood of the victims who had jumped or fallen.

Doctors, nurses, and interns searched each of the bodies on the sidewalk for signs of life, hastily sending off the living in makeshift ambulances and covering the dead. The crowd of onlookers that had begun gathering when the fire first broke out had swelled to thousands. Frantic family members and friends of Triangle employees started a rush toward the police barricades surrounding the building,

A policeman surveys devastation in the street outside the Asch Building.

and the situation threatened to become a riot. Police struggled to keep the crowd back and exhorted the frightened people to be patient.

The bodies of victims were gently laid out on a large square of canvas in the street, where they awaited coffins. Policemen picked up personal items scattered on the sidewalk—coins, handbags, buttons, rosary beads, shoes. Firemen entered the building to search for more victims and, they hoped, more survivors. On the upper floors they were greeted with scenes of utter horror: 13 bodies lying near a flimsy partition on the ninth floor; 20 more lying behind a locked door; other bodies burned to bare bones, skeletons bending over sewing machines.

As evening neared, the firemen wrapped these bodies in nets or tarpaulins and lowered them from the upper windows to the street. A searchlight followed each bundle's descent, and firemen stationed on each floor leaned out of windows to steer the bodies clear of ledges. The "hellish performance," as author Leon Stein describes it, "was greeted only by the wailing of the bereaved men and women and children who had come to search for their own."

Sometime after 8:00 P.M., rescue workers found a survivor in the flooded basement of the building. Herman Meshel had broken through the glass of the eighth-floor elevator door and had then tried to lower himself to safety using the car's cable. But he had fainted and in falling had landed at the bottom of the elevator shaft under the car. After he came to, Meshel heard the sound of water filling the basement and struggled to climb out. But flames in the shaft forced him back into the water, where he remained, freezing and close to drowning, until rescuers found him. After he was taken to safety, firemen set pumps in the basement to empty it.

The grisly chore of searching for bodies continued until 11:30 P.M. Wagons carried bodies in coffins to a temporary morgue on the East 26th Street pier. Homeless men staying in the nearby Municipal Lodging House were pressed into service to unload the corpses. Badly burned bodies were left in the coffins; others were removed and wrapped in sheets, and the coffins sent back to the disaster site. Still, there were not enough coffins for all of the victims, so a ferry was dispatched to Blackwell's Island (in the East River) to bring more from the carpenter's shop at Metropolitan Hospital.

Family members perform the gruesome and heartbreaking task of identifying the bodies of their loved ones. Many victims were burned beyond recognition and had to be identified by their personal effects.

At a police station near the scene, frantic, searching relatives and friends crowded in and gave the names of those they sought. They were directed to the hospital, if they were lucky—or to the morgue, if they were not. One historian describes the awful circuit that friends and relatives traced as they tried to learn the whereabouts of their loved ones: "Toward midnight, many of the stricken moved dazedly . . . from Washington Place, to Mercer Street [Police] Station, to the morgue on 26th Street, and then back to Washington Place." By the morning of March 26, these weary, desperate people were easy to recognize among the throngs of curious onlookers.

That Sunday morning, after water in the basement had been pumped out, two more horribly mangled bodies were discovered. They were women who had crashed through the cellar skylight underneath the fire escape. They were identifiable only by their jewelry.

Police had barricaded the entire block on which the Asch Building stood, and as the morning wore on they kept the growing crowds moving. They later estimated that more than 50,000 people passed by, both the curious and the grief stricken, in a solemn procession that continued for hours. Enterprising individuals peddled apples and pretzels to the crowd, which included busloads of "gaily dressed men and women" from uptown who seemed to view the tragedy as something of a street fair. Others, in shameful displays of profiteering, sold cheap rings and fake jewels that they claimed had been removed from victims' bodies.

From Saturday to Sunday, police struggled to impose order on the chaotic scene at the morgue, too. Small objects, money, or jewelry found on the victims was placed in numbered envelopes corresponding to numbers on the coffins. Organizing this system took all day. Fifty-six of the 136 bodies recovered by that time had been mutilated or burned beyond recognition.

Late Saturday night, close to midnight, authorities had begun admitting small groups of the waiting crowd into the building. Those searching for family and friends cried out and several fainted at the sight of so many victims. Some of them, overcome with grief, ran to the edge of the pier to throw themselves into the river, but vigilant policemen and morgue attendants stopped them. The attendants carried gas lanterns to help light the area as people searched. When a body was identified, attendants would close the coffin and write the name of the deceased on a card attached to the lid, while nurse trainees would comfort the bereaved.

Many victims had been wearing gold jewelry or carrying cash. Sometimes their names were on the pay envelopes they had stuffed into pockets or stockings. One woman victim had $852 in her stocking; to prevent thievery, police were especially careful about who could claim the woman's remains. Another woman, her family complained, was missing not only the shoe in which she kept her money but also several pieces of jewelry.

The bereaved were not the only ones to view the bodies of the victims. A number of fashionably dressed people with no relation to the victims also waited in line. Even as more victims were identified, the crowd did not diminish, and the police found themselves having to keep an eye on shifty pickpockets who had come solely to rob the corpses or members of the waiting crowd. Finally, a deputy police commissioner ordered that anyone unable to provide a name and description of the person they sought was to be turned away immediately. Although the crowd abated, it still numbered several hundred after curious onlookers departed.

Some had more than one victim to identify. Dominick Leone sought no less than three cousins and a niece. Another searcher, Serafino Maltese, identified his 20-year-old and 14-year-old sisters before he fainted. When he recovered, he resumed his search— this time for his mother.

By Sunday evening, an estimated 100,000 people had walked through the morgue. At midnight, many of the identified bodies and 55 nameless ones were transferred from the makeshift morgue to the official one nearby. The identifications proceeded. Family members strained to remember unimportant details about their loved ones that could now be vital in identifying their bodies. One man traveled from Hoboken, New Jersey, to find his 16-year-old daughter, and he was able to recognize her only by a distinctive stitch on the heel of her shoe, which he had recently had repaired. Another man brought with him a pair of shoes just like those he remembered his sister having purchased. He used the new pair to identify his sister.

By Monday morning, more than 40 bodies had been identified. By Tuesday night, 28 bodies still remained unidentified. One coffin contained only a skull and some charred bones. Another held two burned bodies—friends who had died with their arms around each other.

Because some of the bodies were so badly burned, the entire identification process took nearly two weeks. One woman was identified only after a friend brought the victim's dentist to the morgue to examine her teeth. A young girl was identified after her mother recognized a darn in her stocking. Others were identified only by initials engraved on their rings or pocket watches: one woman realized that her fiancé was dead when she saw her own portrait inside his watch. At the end of the week, seven victims remained unidentified: numbers 46, 50, 61, 95, 103, 115, and 127. (One of these was Catherine Maltese, the mother of Serafino Maltese. She was identified in December 1911, nine months after the fire, when her husband managed to recall that a small object at the police station had belonged to her.)

Amid this horror, which several newspapers reported as it was happening, many New Yorkers sadly remembered the 1909-10 strike and the optimism it had sparked among factory workers. William Shepherd, the *New York World* reporter who had witnessed the tragedy, remarked in his article that he "looked upon the heap of dead bodies and I remembered these girls were the shirtwaist makers. I remembered their great strike of last year in which these same girls had demanded more sanitary conditions and more safety precautions in the shops. These dead bodies were the answer." Rosey Safran, a survivor of the fire, recalled the strikers' demands for unlocked doors and better fire escapes. "The bosses defeated us and we didn't get the open doors or the large fire escapes," she wrote, "and so our friends are dead and relatives are tearing their hair."

Perhaps the most celebrated remarks were made at a large memorial and protest meeting held by the WTUL at the Metropolitan Opera House on April 3, 1911. One of the speakers at this meeting was Rose Schneiderman, an immigrant worker and union activist who had helped lead the strike. Schneiderman rose to speak, and with difficulty she controlled the emotion in her voice:

> I would be a traitor to these poor burned bodies if I came here to talk of good fellowship. We have tried you good people of the public and we have found you wanting. . . . This is not the first time girls have been burned alive in this city. Every week I must learn of the untimely death of one of my sister workers. Every year thousands of us are maimed. The life of men and women is so cheap and property is so sacred. There are so many of us [competing] for one job [that] it mat-

ters little if 140-odd are burned to death.

We have tried you, citizens; we are trying you now, and you have a couple of dollars for the sorrowing mothers and daughters and sisters by way of a charity gift. But every time the workers come out in the only way they know to protest against conditions which are unbearable, the strong hand of the law is allowed to press down heavily upon us. . . .

I can't talk fellowship to you who are gathered here. Too much blood has been spilled. I know from my experience that it is up to the working people to save themselves. The only way they can save themselves is by a strong working-class movement.

The meeting at which Schneiderman spoke these powerful words helped organize workers and reformers to attack unsanitary and unsafe working conditions by getting new laws passed. The Factory Investigating Commission (FIC) was formed a short time after this mass meeting, and it held its first hearings in October 1911.

But before the FIC could even begin its investigation, before the working conditions that led to tragedy could be rectified, the victims and survivors and their families needed immediate help. In the aftermath of the tragedy, the American Red Cross, the ILGWU, and the WTUL organized a relief effort. The hearts of the citizens of New York and of other American cities and towns went out to the fire victims and their families. By March 31—just six days after the blaze—the relief fund

"In Compliance with Law?" read the original caption of this cartoon, which appeared in the *New York Tribune*. In the wake of the Triangle disaster, many people wondered how a building with a fire escape that ended at the second floor could be in compliance with building codes.

"The life of men and women is so cheap and property is so sacred," declared union activist Rose Schneiderman after the Triangle disaster. "I know from my experience that it is up to the working people to save themselves . . . by a strong working-class movement."

had already reached $65,000; by April 5 the total was $80,000. Another organization, the Charities Organization Society, coordinated the efforts of a number of private relief agencies to prevent overlap.

In the weeks immediately following the fire, the Red Cross itself offered small amounts of money to the victims' families as temporary relief to cover incidental expenses and loss of income, at a total of more than $12,000; another $6,000 helped cover funeral expenses. The Red Cross also established a number of trust funds for the dependent children of some of the fire victims.

In addition, the Red Cross also gave tens of thousands of dollars to families that had been dependent on fire victims' incomes, whether or not the families lived in the United States. More than $44,000 went to U.S.

families, and $17,000 went to those living overseas—in Palestine, Russia, Eastern Europe, and the West Indies—who had relied financially on their relatives in America.

Both the Red Cross and the WTUL emphasized the extreme hardships caused by the loss of income from those who had perished. Their income, both organizations stated, was not merely "pin money." Said one spokeswoman for the WTUL, "These girls, then, just at the age when clothes and good times make their greatest appeal, were not working at a power machine in a high loft building for nothing. They were there because they were the support of a great number of people."

On April 5, by order of the mayor of New York City, the last seven unidentified victims were carried to a cemetery in Brooklyn to be buried. For those who couldn't go to Brooklyn, a memorial march was held at the same time in Manhattan. In pouring rain, more than 120,000 mourners silently marched up Fifth Avenue behind the empty hearse, while thousands more observers lined the street. The procession was led by Rose Schneiderman, who was accompanied by Mary Dreier (the president of the New York WTUL) and Helen Marot (the secretary of the WTUL). The silent cortege deeply affected many spectators. Some marchers carried shirtwaist-workers' banners as memorials to their fallen coworkers and as a protest against the unsafe conditions that had led to their deaths. The marchers were so numerous that it took four hours for all of them to pass under the stately Memorial Arch in Washington Square.

Even before the last body had been removed from the Asch Building on Sunday, March 26, the debate began over who was to blame for a fire that could claim so many lives in just 30 minutes. City officials and politicians were understandably appalled—yet each of them placed the responsibility on others. Such divisiveness extended even to the official inquiries into the cause of the blaze. Four separate investigations were launched by the city coroner, the district attorney, Fire Commissioner Rhinelander Waldo, and Acting Building Superintendent Albert Ludwig.

At the same time, newspapers echoed the outrage of their readers. Printed political cartoons and editorials demanded that the guilty be punished. One cartoon showed a horrifying drawing of women plummeting from a collapsing fire escape and landing on iron pilings; the caption read, "In Compliance with Law?" Another was a drawing of a gallows with the caption, "This Ought to Fit Somebody; Who Is He?"

The city coroner and district attorney laid blame on the New York City Building Department. The Building Department claimed that the Asch Building was fireproof and that the department had no power of enforcement. (The superintendent of buildings in Manhattan at this time was the same man who in 1901 had criticized the plans for the Asch Building.) The state Department of Labor also reported that it had investigated Triangle and found it to be in compliance with current laws. One of its inspectors had given the Triangle factory a passing evaluation only a month before the fire.

The New York City Fire Department, too, was blamed for not forwarding any reports on Triangle or the Asch Building to the city Building Department. Fire Chief Edward Croker declared, "I have been

arguing, complaining, and grumbling about . . . [fire escapes] for a long time." Croker insisted that his warnings had either been defeated or ignored. Governor John Alden Dix of New York even tried to blame the victims, claiming that because they had not properly familiarized themselves with their workplace, they did not know in advance which exits they should use during an emergency.

In reality, the city departments shared the blame for the tragedy. Chief Croker angrily complained, "Those responsible for buildings include the Tenement House Department, the Factory Inspection Department, the Building Department, the Health Department, the Department of Water Supply, Gas and Electricity and the Police Department to see that the orders of the other five departments are carried out." Yet, he continued, the Fire Department itself was not permitted to rule on fire

On April 5, 1911—an appropriately dreary day—120,000 people in Manhattan participated in a memorial march for the Triangle Shirtwaist fire victims.

escapes or fire exits.

Some observers noted that of all the buildings on Washington Place, only the Asch Building even had a fire escape. Others pointed out that Triangle, which hired multilingual employees, had never had a fire drill or posted placards detailing escape routes. The problems were many. Lillian Wald of the Joint Board of Sanitary Control fumed, "The crux of the situation is that there is no direct responsibility. Divided, always divided! The responsibility rests nowhere!"

As an immediate result of the Triangle fire, several new city laws were enacted regarding fire safety in all buildings (not just factories). In October 1911, the city of New York passed the Sullivan-Hoey Act, which established a Bureau of Fire Prevention, expanded the powers of the Fire Commissioner, and ended the confusion over which city departments were responsible for detecting safety violations.

In the years after the Triangle tragedy, New York City also revised its building code to include more protection against fires. All elements of new buildings had to be fireproof, including doors, windows, and trim. Owners of older buildings that were not fireproof were required to make specific improvements: they had to install fireproof stairwells with fire partitions extending all the way from the floor to the roof of the building. Structures higher than 85 feet were required to have at least one fireproof stairway, with doors leading to the stairway either from outside balconies or from fireproof vestibules. In any building in which large numbers of people would be working, the owners and proprietors were to install fire alarms, extinguishers, hoses, and fire doors. All combustible materials had to be stored in a safe place, surrounded by fire-retardant materials. Waste materials were to be removed daily. And perhaps most important, smoking—an often cited cause of fires—was banned in all parts of all factory buildings.

The Fire Commission also recommended changes in building regulations. It required that all doors open outward and sprinklers be installed in any building higher than seven stories. In companies employing more than 25 workers, the commission required that fire drills be conducted at least once every three months. Occupancy limits and "no smoking" signs were to be posted where all could read them.

Although many felt justice for the victims of the Triangle fire was obtained when New York City passed such fire codes, others believed the new regulations were merely rudimentary. Much more needed to be done to prevent another tragedy like the Triangle fire. Reformers and labor leaders focused their energies on the state legislature—and on changing the laws that allowed employers to exploit workers through unfair business practices.

The owners of the Triangle Shirtwaist Company were not alone in their negligence of employee safety and health. Had the disastrous fire not happened at Triangle, it would probably have happened somewhere else. But the tragedy shocked and horrified not only the city and the state of New York but also the rest of the nation. The investigations, inspections, and legal trial that followed the disaster awakened Americans not only to the importance of fire prevention measures, but also to the plight of factory workers—and to the necessity of better laws to ensure the safety of their workplaces.

The Shirtwaist Kings: Business as Usual

Deathtrap: the Triangle factory floor after the devastating fire.

6

Blame for the tragic loss of life in the Triangle Fire did not rest only with the New York City government. Yet the actions taken by the building and company owners after the fire demonstrated their lack of concern.

While debris was still being cleared from the Asch Building after the fire, Joseph Asch applied for a new building permit to refurbish the structure. The application requested permission to restore the building to its original condition—no improvements were intended!

And Max Blanck and Isaac Harris, the owners of the Triangle Company, placed advertisements in New York newspapers the Monday after the fire to inform their customers that they were open for business in a new office. A few days after the fire, too, they advertised that they were hiring new workers! Such actions infuriated many in New York City, not to mention the survivors and the victims' families. Several newspapers refused to run Triangle's ads.

The Building Department immediately investigated the Triangle owners' new shop. They found several violations. The new shop was on the top floor of a six-story building, which itself was unsafe for use as a factory; it was not fireproof, it didn't have enough exits, and there were no fire escapes. Tables and machinery were densely packed in the new shop; a garment worker would not have been able to stand up without disrupting other employees. Essentially the Triangle partners, despite having witnessed the deaths of so many of their employees, assumed they could return to business as usual.

On April 11, 1911, Harris and Blanck were indicted on 46 counts of first- and second-degree manslaughter by a New York City grand jury. The charges rested mostly on one slender claim. The indictment alleged that Harris and Blanck were responsible for the death of at least one of their employees because they had ordered a door on the ninth floor to be locked. The state labor code required that all factory doors remain unlocked during business hours. Keeping a door locked was a misdemeanor, but if someone died as a result of that misdemeanor, the person who committed it was guilty of manslaughter—a felony.

To prove the case, the prosecution had to show three things: that a certain door was locked, that Harris and Blanck knew it was locked (or had ordered it to be locked), and that someone had died as a direct result

TRIANGLE SHIRT WAIST MANUFACTURERS
LISTENING TO TESTIMONY AGAINST THEM

MAX BLANCK   ISAAC HARRIS

Max Blanck and Isaac Harris, the owners of Triangle, are depicted at their manslaughter trial in this drawing from the *New York World*. On December 28, 1911, the two were acquitted.

of that locked door. Prosecutors chose to focus on one young victim, Margaret Swartz (sometimes spelled Schwartz), whose body had been among 20 found behind a locked door on the ninth floor. Two witnesses had seen Swartz attempting to open the door, and one had actually heard her scream that the door was locked as her dress and hair caught fire.

Yet the prosecution had a difficult case. The piles of flammable scraps lying around the Triangle factory, the overcrowding that made escape difficult or impossible, and the unsanitary conditions at the factory were irrelevant to the legal case because those conditions were not against the law. The prosecution needed to establish that Margaret Swartz had died because her employers had ordered that the ninth-floor door where she perished be kept locked.

Although the trial began eight months after the fire, emotions still ran high. The families of victims and survivors crowded the courtroom and demonstrated outside the court building. On December 5, Harris and Blanck were accosted on their way into the court building by 300 enraged women shouting, "Murderers! Kill the murderers!"

As the law stood at the time, an employer's rights were more important than those of his employees. It was believed that employees assumed the risks associated with a job when they agreed to work, and could not, then, hold their employers liable for injury or even death occurring on the job. Workers' compensation, an insurance system that helps pay employees for job-related injuries, did not yet exist. And in 1911 injured employees or their surviving families won very few cases against employers in civil court.

Harris and Blanck were represented by an excellent lawyer, Max Steuer. He had grown up in the Lower East Side, an immigrant neighborhood that had been home to many of the victims. His cross-examination of some of the witnesses was so brilliant that it is still cited as an example to law students. He sought to prove that the door was not locked, or that Harris and Blanck had not known it was locked. He sought to show the jury that workers were able to steal the owners' property by smuggling shirtwaists out in their handbags. Thus, Steuer claimed, Harris and Blanck were justified in locking all the doors but one at quitting time, forcing their workers to go through one narrow doorway and have their bags searched by a watchman one at a time.

(On further questioning, Harris admitted that the total amount stolen from him in several years of business would not have exceeded $25.)

The judge, too, instructed the jury that "you must find that this door was locked. If it was locked and locked with the knowledge of the defendants, you must also find beyond reasonable doubt that such locking caused the death of Margaret Schwartz."

Many jury members could not be sure that Harris and Blanck knew the door was locked. As a result, the Triangle owners were acquitted on December 28, 1911. Although New York State did bring charges against Harris and Blanck in the name of another fire victim in March 1912, it was subsequently ruled that such action would constitute "double jeopardy," or trying a person more than once for the same crime without any new evidence. Double jeopardy is illegal in the United States.

The acquittal of the Triangle Company owners angered many people nationwide. Because no one was held directly accountable for the fire, public opinion began to grow in support of the cause of labor unions. "The events of 1911 seem to have made [people] more keenly aware than they had ever been that the workers' fight for reform was absolutely essential," writes author Bonnie Mitelman.

In 1912, the Factory Investigating Commission made its first report. Funded by the state of New York, the commission did not seek simply to lay blame or to prevent other fires. Instead, its purpose was to investigate all dangerous and unfair conditions that harmed workers. The FIC, says author Thomas Kerr, "assembled the most extensive wage study in the country and

Franklin Delano Roosevelt (second from left) and Alfred E. Smith (fourth from left) were members of a blue-ribbon commission set up to investigate factory conditions after the Triangle fire. Concern for the plight of workers would figure in both men's later political careers—Smith as governor of New York, and Roosevelt as U.S. president.

introduced into public debate the reformers' minimum-wage arguments."

The commission enlisted the support of many labor organizations, and its members included several people who would become famous in later years. Al Smith, later governor of New York and a presidential candidate, and Robert Wagner, a state senator, were on the commission. So was Frances Perkins, a worker for the National Consumers League, which pledged to boycott clothing made in unsanitary and dangerous shops. Perkins later became the U.S. secretary of labor, the first woman to be appointed to a president's cabinet. Another state senator appointed to the FIC was Franklin Delano Roosevelt, who went on to become the governor of New York and the only four-term president of the United States. The Triangle fire and the conditions that led to the tragic loss of life were pivotal in the political lives of these reformers.

As early as May 1911, the FIC had investigated 1,836 factories in 20 separate industries. The FIC's reports spurred the passage of 8 new state labor laws in 1912, an additional 25 in 1913, and 3 more in 1914.

One law increased the number of Labor Department inspectors and almost doubled the department's budget. Another allowed for stricter punishments for violators of the labor code. A third required that buildings constructed as warehouses be modified for safety before being converted to factories. And yet another law made it illegal for children under 14 to work in factories.

The FIC had many prominent staff members who had declined receiving a salary. When the commission was dissolved in 1915, after three and a half years of work, the FIC had cost the state only $110,000. Many reformers agreed with Frances Perkins, who said that the FIC's work marked "a turning point in American attitudes and policies toward social responsibility." According to a study by Frances B. Jensen, the FIC's efforts produced "the most advanced and comprehensive standards in the nation." Until Franklin D. Roosevelt's New Deal programs and federal legislation in the 1930s (including the Wagner Act), these new standards in New York State were the model followed by all other states.

Not everyone, of course, abided by the new laws. To many it must have seemed that even when factory conditions and fire laws were changed, Harris and Blanck still had not learned the lesson of the fire. One might think that after the overwhelmingly negative publicity, they might have left the business or moved to another city; at the very least, that they might have changed their ways. Apparently this was not the case.

After the tragic fire, Harris and Blanck hired a firm called Goldstein and Company as an insurance adjuster to help them obtain their insurance money. Triangle had carried $174,750 in insurance on stock and $25,000 on furniture. There was no proof, says one author, that the actual value of the company was more than $134,000, at the most. And the account books had been destroyed in the fire. Still, all but one of the 37 companies that had underwritten Triangle's insurance policies paid out the claim. As early as October 1911, Harris and Blanck filed suit against the remaining company for nonpayment. By May 1913, Triangle's owners had collected $190,000 in insurance claims, the largest payout in New York history up to that time. Goldstein and Company's fee was $8,500.

In September 1913, Max Blanck was fined for violating the labor code. An inspector had found that one of the doors in Blanck's shop was locked with a chain during working hours. Again, on December 1, 1913, Blanck was fined for a different labor violation.

On December 23, Blanck invited several city officials to view a demonstration of a new lock being tested at his shop. Not only did the officials find the lock inadequate for safety, they were distracted by six-foot-high piles of waste, the use of wicker baskets instead of metal boxes, and cramped conditions in the shop. The Bureau of Fire Prevention sternly warned Blanck to fix the safety violations.

In March 1914, the National Consumers League

(NCL) complained that Triangle was producing garments that carried a counterfeit of the league's label. The NCL label was given only to factories whose shops were certified as "clean and healthful." When consumers saw the NCL label on a garment, they would know the product was from a certified shop, and by buying it they would be supporting workers' safety. Triangle was slapped with a court injunction to stop it from using the counterfeit label, but the company was not otherwise punished.

Just three days before the court injunction was served, 23 families of fire victims, who had been waiting three years for reparations, settled their insurance claims with the building owner, Joseph Asch. As the *New York World* reported, "the claimants have been tired out. Their money and their patience have been exhausted." The payment averaged about $75 per life. The *New York Post* caustically wrote, "It seemed little enough, but, to be sure, they could console themselves with the thought that it was nearly four times as much as the $20 fine which [was] imposed upon Max Blanck . . . two and a half years after the fire, for keeping the door of another factory locked."

Decades later, as the 47th anniversary of the Triangle fire approached, author Leon Stein was at the scene of a fire in the Monarch Undergarment Factory, located at 623 Broadway, New York. Six stories high, the 77-year-old building had no sprinklers and a useless fire escape. A fire drill had never been held.

> In the middle of the floor areas were glass blocks, overlaid with wood in some forgotten and unrecorded time when the structure was converted from a warehouse to

a factory building. The fire had started on the third floor in a textile finishing firm using an oven box which blew up. It burned for seven minutes before an alarm was turned in—from the street. Almost until that moment, the workers on the fourth floor, busy making women's undergarments in a clean, well-run union shop, were unaware of the hell burning beneath them. Then the smoke came. A courageous boss cautioned against panic, stayed with his workers, died with them. For soon the glass blocks worked loose and the entire middle section of the fourth floor collapsed—flat, like a falling pancake. Twenty-four died.

Josephine Nicolosi, a survivor of the Triangle fire, lived nearby. Seeing the smoke, she ran outside and watched, horrified, as the bodies were removed from the building. According to her friend Leon Stein, "She gripped me by the wrists and shaking me demanded with anger and despair: 'What good have been all the years? The fire still burns!'"

Indeed, as Stein himself notes, a bill was passed by the state legislature of New York in 1961 that would have canceled out the overdue safety measures passed after the Monarch fire. All Americans need to be aware of the dangers of "backsliding" on safety legislation. Laws can be repealed, sometimes quietly without much protest or even attention. Sometimes laws are enforced only half-heartedly. And industry leaders often fund lobbyists at local, state, and federal government levels to protect business interests and try to stop legislation that will lower company profits. Industry interests have the money and the time to spend on protecting themselves, sometimes at the expense of

workers and consumers.

The fire like the one at Triangle can happen again. In May 1993, more than 200 workers were killed in the world's worst factory fire, in Bangkok, Thailand. To prevent theft by workers, officials at Kader Industrial Company had ordered its security guards to lock all the doors except one, as soon as all workers had entered the building in the morning. After the fire was discovered, panicked workers fled to the one open staircase, where "they met department chiefs who tried to block them from fleeing, threatening them with dismissal," one journalist reported.

When they realized that the other exits were

Fire department officials examine the scene of a 1958 garment factory fire that claimed the lives of 24 persons. Though building codes have been tightened considerably since the Triangle fire, worker safety can never be taken for granted.

Coworkers and emergency personnel treat victims of a fire at the Imperial Food Products plant in Hamlet, North Carolina, September 4, 1991. As with the Triangle disaster 80 years earlier, many of the 25 people killed in the Imperial fire may have died because management had locked doors in order to prevent theft.

locked, hundreds jumped out the windows from the third and fourth floors. There were no fire alarms and no fire escapes, despite an earlier fire at the plant in 1989. One hundred eighty-two bodies were found near the one staircase the workers could use. More than 500 people were hospitalized.

Deadly factory fires still occur in the United States as well. In September 1991, a fire broke out at an Imperial Foods plant in Hamlet, North Carolina. Twenty-five workers died because here, too, the doors were locked in violation of fire safety laws. Another 40 people were injured. Fires had broken out at the plant before, in 1980 and in 1983. Despite this, in the Hamlet plant's 11 years of operation, it had never once been inspected by North Carolina's Department of Labor. After the 1991 fire, the plant was cited for at least 83 workplace-safety violations.

The Asch Building still stands, although it has been heavily refurbished. New York University acquired the building in 1929, and it now houses several University departments. A plaque on the outside wall memorializes the fire victims. It reads, in part, "Out of their martyrdom came new concepts of social responsibility and labor legislation that have helped make American working conditions the finest in the world."

"The Finest in the World"?

Razor wire surrounds an apartment complex in El Monte, California, where 56 Thai immigrants were held in virtual slavery, forced to sew clothing that their captors in turn sold.

7

Aurora Blancas worked in a garment factory in New York City. "I started working the same day I asked for the job. The boss asked me my name and how old I was. Nothing more," she said. Blancas toiled 11 hours a day, six days a week in a dirty, crowded shop. And when payday arrived, her boss frequently refused to pay her. Though Blancas tried to get her coworkers to speak up about the unfair conditions, they were too afraid. So she took it upon herself to report the garment factory to union officials—and was promptly fired.

Another garment worker, Bertha Morales, was shocked at what went on at her workplace. Morales saw her boss hit one worker for making a mistake. A second had her hair yanked. A third was fired because she yawned.

Although these incidents might seem like scenes from a bygone era, they all happened in the 1990s. "Sweatshops" are back. Commenting on this disturbing trend, U.S. secretary of labor Robert Reich said in 1996, "These are the kinds of conditions we haven't seen since the turn of the century."

As defined by the U.S. government's General Accounting Office, a sweatshop is "an employer who violates more than one federal or state labor law governing minimum wage and overtime, child labor, industrial homework, occupational safety and health, workers' compensation or industry registration," or an employer who violates one law chronically. Under such a definition, the U.S. Department of Labor estimates that there may be as many as 13,000 sweatshops in America. Most are in the garment industry.

Nearly all employees of American sweatshops are immigrants, and close to 80 percent are women, just as they were at Triangle and other shops in the early 1900s. The conditions they toil under are as bad as or worse than those that existed at Triangle. In addition to dirty, dangerous shops, "physical abuse is unfortunately quite common, and there's always the yelling," says a spokesperson for the Union of Needletrades, Industrial and Textile Employees, or UNITE. (UNITE was formed in 1995 when the International Ladies Garment Workers Union and the Amalgamated Clothing and Textile Workers Union merged into one union.) Instead of being from eastern Europe, Russia, or Italy, today's sweatshop workers are more often from Asia, Central America, or Mexico. One other difference: many sweatshops today are owned by other immigrants.

How can such a situation exist at the dawn of the 21st century in the United States, where labor laws and inspectors are supposed to protect workers from exploitation? One reason is that there are still not enough inspectors to investigate about 22,000 sewing businesses in the United States, an estimated half of which violate laws concerning minimum wage and overtime. Labor inspectors, too, have many facilities to inspect besides those in the garment industry, and the number of inspectors was drastically reduced in the 1980s under the administration of President Ronald Reagan.

Another reason for the continued existence of sweatshops in the 1990s is that the employees themselves often make inspectors' jobs more difficult.

The nationalities of the workers and the clothing styles may have changed, but conditions in this modern-day sweatshop aren't much different from conditions in the sweatshops of the early 20th century.

Because most people employed in sweatshops are illegal aliens—immigrants not properly registered with the U.S. government—they are afraid they will be deported if officials find out they are illegal residents. As bad as their current situation is, conditions in their country of origin were often worse. This makes the workers less likely to cooperate with the very officials who can help them. Often, too, the workers don't speak English and can't easily communicate with authorities, and they fear retribution by their employers if they do complain.

The secrecy in some shops, said one labor official, "is almost impossible to break unless the shop goes out of business." But, investigators say, even when caught most owners just open up again in a new place, under a different name—often after having cheated their former workers out of thousands of dollars in back wages.

Beyond the problem of illegal aliens and the scarcity of labor investigators, fundamental economic changes over the past several decades have provided a fertile field for the growth of sweatshops. During the 1950s and 1960s, labor unions hit their peak membership and exerted a good deal of influence over the garment industry. But in later decades, with the growth of the global economy, the power of unions has declined. American clothing manufacturers began to face stiff competition from companies around the world, which could offer their products at much lower prices because their costs—particularly their labor costs—were much lower. A garment worker in Central America, the Caribbean, or Asia, for example, might be paid in a week the wage a U.S. worker earned in an *hour*. To take advantage of these dramatically lower labor costs,

many U.S. companies decided to move their manufac-
turing facilities overseas. Those that didn't move had to
find some other way to reduce labor costs or increase
workers' productivity in order to stay in business.

During the past 30 years, the U.S. market for clothing has become increasingly dominated by chain stores.
Today, these major retailers control 80 percent of the
American clothing market. The large retailers order
shipments of garments from manufacturers, about
1,000 of which are located in the United States. Most of
these manufacturers hire contractors to actually make
the garments, and the contractors themselves often use
subcontractors. In total, the garment-manufacturing
industry in the United States comprises about 22,000
contractors and subcontractors, and most of the sweatshops are in this group.

Although labor costs are generally much lower in
countries such as China and Mexico, sometimes it can
still be economical for retailers to turn to American, or
domestic, garment makers. Because major retailers
use computerized inventory systems to keep track of
their merchandise, they can avoid carrying large
amounts of inventory. But this means that when the
retailers do need a product, the manufacturers must
fill the orders rapidly, often in just a few weeks.
Because shops located in the United States require less
shipping time, they have a natural advantage by pro-
viding quick turnaround. But as foreign manufacturers have sped up their production, the American
shops' advantage has largely disappeared. The slightly
longer turnaround time of foreign shops is offset by
dramatically lower labor costs, so many retailers and
manufacturers are increasingly looking to overseas

businesses to fill garment orders.

To remain competitive, many American companies that have kept their operations in the United States have lowered pay rates for piecework and for regular employees. And inevitably, many manufacturers have hired contractors or subcontractors—either knowingly or unknowingly—that are sweatshops. One garment manufacturer explained what has happened in the industry over the past few decades this way:

> It used to be most manufacturers would have their own factories and maybe it cost them $3 to produce a garment because they wanted to play by the rules. But then the retailer found he can go out into the infrastructure of labor and get the price down to $2.50 or $2—and a lot of the legitimate manufacturers gave up. They sent the order to a contractor, who could get the price down because he didn't play by the rules. The moral fiber broke down and it became a free-for-all.

Evidence of this moral free-for-all can be found in the heartbreaking stories of immigrants trapped in a kind of slavery, called "debt bondage," in the United States. Smugglers offer to bring undocumented aliens to America and find them jobs, for a fee. Once in America, these illegal immigrants become virtual slaves to the smugglers or their agents or bosses. People are kept against their will, forced to work literally for pennies to pay off their debts. An estimated 10,000 Chinese immigrants alone are illegally smuggled into the United States every year—at a fee of up to $30,000 each. Chinese gangs, authorities believe, have developed particularly well-organized ways to smuggle immigrants, but illegal aliens also arrive from other

parts of Asia, Central and South America, and the Caribbean. Many of these unfortunate people, who hoped for a better life in the United States, end up threatened, beaten, stabbed, raped, and even sold into prostitution. Authorities fear that the problem is more widespread than the public can imagine. In other words, slavery still exists in the United States.

The existence of sweatshops in this country garnered a great deal of public attention after government officials raided a company in El Monte, California, in 1995. Inside an apartment complex surrounded by razor wire, labor investigators discovered 68 workers from Thailand. Neighbors of the sweatshop had no idea what was happening inside the owners' well-kept

Masked protesters take TV personality Kathie Lee Gifford to task for the sweatshop conditions under which her line of apparel was allegedly made. In today's garment industry, there is no guarantee that a piece of clothing sold in a reputable store came from a legitimate factory.

property, because the workers had never been allowed outside. They sewed clothing for at least 17 hours a day, and sometimes up to 22 hours, earning about 69 cents an hour. They slept on the floor and were beaten regularly. Their wages, they had hoped, would pay off the $4,800 debt each owed for being brought to the United States. But some of them had been forced to continue working even after their debts had been paid.

As a result of this high-profile case, the federal government launched a task force to uncover and punish sweatshop owners and those who profited from them. The Thai sweatshop in El Monte held invoices for 18 major retailers, who may or may not have known of the conditions under which workers sewed their clothing.

Yet another well-publicized case involved Kathie Lee Gifford, a talk-show host who has her own line of clothing. In 1996 Gifford was targeted by the media after it was reported to the U.S. government that some of her clothing items were made by children in Honduras earning as little as 30 cents an hour. Gifford has since become an outspoken advocate of better conditions for garment workers. Many retailers, too, have pledged to investigate their contractors and to cooperate fully with authorities when violations are discovered.

There is little doubt that it is the large companies that can bring about change in the way garment workers are treated. Because these large firms control most of the U.S. market, they are often able to set prices and demand fast turnaround. "If you have 10,000 stores, each ordering small quantities, they don't have much leverage," one manufacturer explains. "If you have a couple retailers ordering the equivalent of 10,000 stores, they can leverage anything."

Although big retailers and manufacturers have some leverage in determining prices (and therefore wages), they are also driven by market forces. Consumers demand quality clothing, footwear, bags, and other items at very low prices. In this sense, then, it's up to consumers to put pressure on manufacturers to stop sweatshops from profiting. One way is to refuse to buy from companies who use sweatshop labor.

In a 1995 poll conducted by Marymount University in Maryland, 78 percent of respondents said they would avoid stores selling items made in sweatshops—if they knew which stores they were. And 84 percent said they would pay slightly more for a garment known to be manufactured under safe and legal working conditions.

A big stumbling block to any effective consumer action has been that consumers have no way of knowing whether their clothes and other items were made by law-abiding companies or under sweatshop conditions. To remedy that situation, the U.S. Department of Labor launched a campaign in 1996 for a "No Sweat" label that could be sewn into clothing to certify its origin in a clean, law-abiding shop. The department also began publicizing the names of shops and contractors known to have violated wage and hours laws, so that consumers would know which companies to avoid.

A label is a good start, as long as the public remembers that it's only a start, say advocates for garment workers. But other groups are also making advances in the fight to abolish sweatshops in the United States. The government task force formed after the El Monte incident included human rights groups, labor unions, and several large apparel companies. In 1997 the task force

Brown University students protest the school's association with companies reportedly using sweatshop labor. Consumer awareness and action may hold the best hope for ensuring that clothing makers treat their employees fairly.

instituted a voluntary code of conduct for manufacturers. The code should apply both to U.S. factories and to those overseas, where abuses are even more rampant because of lax laws and corruption.

The New York State Labor-Religion Coalition (NYSLRC) launched a three-year program in late 1998. The group seeks to target sweatshop manufacture of school and university logo apparel, which in America has become a $2.5 billion industry. The campaign encourages schools to investigate the manufacturers and contractors from which they order such items. Several large universities have also adopted codes of conduct for the manufacturers who supply uniforms and items displaying school logos. In several cases, stricter codes were adopted after student protests—notably at the University of Wisconsin, in Madison; Georgetown University, in Washington, D.C.; and Duke University, in Durham, North Carolina. The success of these protests indicates that in some cases, change does come from "below," and the average citizen can make a difference.

Still, nearly half of the clothing sold in the United States is manufactured in Asia, the Caribbean, and Central and South America. And as U.S. labor officials and other authorities have cracked down on sweatshops in the United States, more and more companies have decided to move their operations overseas. "If we can't eradicate sweatshops and child labor at home, how do you think we're going to do it for Indonesia or Bangladesh?" asks former U.S. secretary of labor John Dunlop.

Legislation restricting immigration or penalizing illegal immigrants does not seem to be working. The federal Immigration Restriction and Control Act, passed in 1986, merely drove illegal immigrants into an "underground economy." Here they remain undocumented, unprotected, and easy prey for unscrupulous employers. Sweatshop employers can and do use the threat of calling the Immigration and Naturalization Service (INS) as a club to keep their workers—who

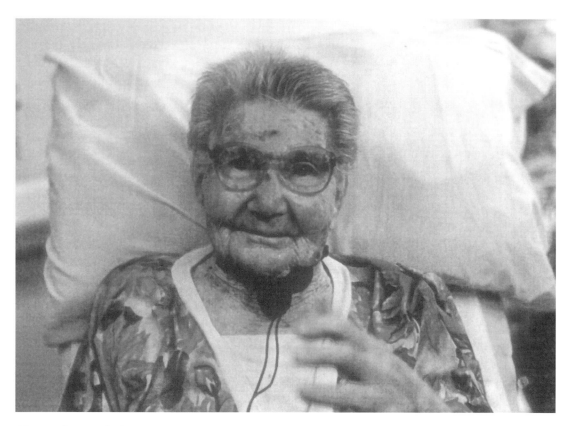

Above: Bessie Cohen, one of the last two known survivors of the Triangle factory fire, died in 1999 at the age of 107. Opposite page: So that future generations would not forget the events of March 25, 1911, the Asch Building was designated a national historic landmark.

fear deportation—in submission.

Alternatively, a pact between the federal Labor Department and the INS in November 1998 may result in the punishment of abusive sweatshop owners, while protecting workers who speak out against them from immediate deportation. According to the terms of the agreement, now when workers inform the Labor Department about workplace abuses, the complaint will not automatically trigger an INS raid.

The Labor Department encourages consumers who want to help abolish sweatshops to do so in the following simple ways: Ask your clothing retailers questions about where the garments were made and by whom. Ask retailers if they monitor their manufacturers. Ask

TRIANGLE SHIRTWAIST FACTORY
(ASCH BUILDING)
HAS BEEN DESIGNATED A
NATIONAL HISTORIC LANDMARK
THE TRIANGLE SHIRTWAIST FACTORY FIRE,
IN WHICH 146 WORKERS DIED,
OCCURRED HERE ON MARCH 25, 1911.
THIS BUILDING POSSESSES NATIONAL SIGNIFICANCE
IN COMMEMORATING THE HISTORY OF THE
UNITED STATES OF AMERICA.
1991
NATIONAL PARK SERVICE
UNITED STATES DEPARTMENT OF THE INTERIOR

if they support "No Sweat" clothing. To help consumers make informed decisions, the U.S. Department of Labor has issued a list of companies that have pledged to eliminate sweatshops, which is available upon request.

In February 1999, one of the two known survivors of the 1911 Triangle Shirtwaist Company fire, Bessie Cohen, died at age 107. As of this writing, Rose Freedman, 105, is the only known living survivor of the fire. Nearly 90 years after that tragic day, it is still important for Americans to remember what happened there and why. There will always be factories, but they don't have to be firetraps. The Triangle factory fire, the most powerful symbol of unfair labor practices and a disregard for worker safety, is also a reminder of what can still happen.

Chronology

1901   Joseph Asch's building on Greene Street and Washington Place completed

1902   Harris and Blanck's business, the Triangle Shirtwaist Company, occupies ninth floor of the Asch building

1906   Harris and Blanck's company expands to include the eighth floor

1908   Triangle Shirtwaist Company's general offices installed on tenth floor

1909   *September:* Local 25 of the International Ladies Garment Workers' Union (ILGWU) declares strike against Triangle

   November: Diamond Company employees strike; at Cooper Union meeting, shirtwaist makers declare general strike; nearly 40,000 participate

   December: Strikers march to New York city hall; Philadelphia shirtwaist workers join strike

1910   *January:* ILGWU calls for arbitration; manufacturers' association refuses

   February: Philadelphia shirtwaist makers end strike; ILGWU declares strike officially over

   December: 1,000 New York City shirtwaist makers strike at 11 firms over refusal to renew union contracts

1911   *March 25:* Triangle Shirtwaist Factory burns; 146 workers perish

   March 28: Women's Trade Union League (WTUL) conducts inquiry into working conditions in factories; 1,000 workers give testimony

   April 5: WTUL and ILGWU lead 120,000 in silent memorial parade for the unidentified Triangle fire victims

   April 11: Triangle owners Harris and Blanck indicted for manslaughter

   October: Sullivan-Hoey Act passed in New York City, establishing Bureau of Fire Prevention and clarifying which departments are responsible for enforcement of building and fire codes

   October 10: New York State Factory Investigating Commission (FIC) opens hearings

October 17: Harris and Blanck sue Royal Insurance Company over nonpayment of fire insurance claim

November 3: Harris and Blanck plead not guilty to manslaughter charge

November 13: Fire survivors march to protest dangerous factory conditions

December 5: Three hundred women attack Harris and Blanck on first day of trial

December 28: Harris and Blanck acquitted

1912 *March 27:* New York State Superior Court dismisses remaining indictments against Harris and Blanck

1913 *February–May:* New York State legislature passes 25 new factory-safety bills

July 31: Bureau of Fire Prevention cites Asch Building for violations

August 2: FIC issues fire safety recommendations

August 20: Max Blanck arraigned in court for keeping a door locked at Triangle's new shop during working hours

December 1: Triangle Shirtwaist Company fined for violations of labor law

December 23: Bureau of Fire Prevention officials find several safety violations at Max Blanck's shop

1914 *March 4:* National Consumers League (NCL) seeks court injunction to prevent Triangle Company from using counterfeit NCL label; 11 claims against owner of Asch building settled for $75 per victim

1958 Fire at Monarch Undergarment Factory in New York City kills 24

1993 World's worst factory fire at Kader Industrial Company, near Bangkok, Thailand, kills more than 200

1995 Federal government begins crackdown on sweatshops in United States

Further Reading

Bader, Bonnie. *East Side Story*. New York: Silver Moon Press, 1993.

Goldin, Barbara Diamond. *Fire! The Beginnings of the Labor Movement*. New York: Puffin Books, 1992.

Lasky, Kathryn. *Dreams in the Golden Country: The Diary of Zipporah Feldman, a Jewish Immigrant Girl, New York City, 1903*. New York: Scholastic, 1998.

Littlefield, Holly. *Fire at the Triangle Factory*. Minneapolis: Carolrhoda Books, 1996.

Malkiel, Theresa S. *The Diary of a Shirtwaist Striker*. Ithaca, New York: Cornell University Press, 1990.

Sherrow, Victoria. *The Triangle Factory Fire*. Brookfield, Conn.: The Millbrook Press, 1995.

Index

Index

Index

GINA DE ANGELIS is a freelance writer living in southern Virginia. She holds a B.A. from Marlboro College and an M.A. from the University of Mississippi. This is her tenth book for Chelsea House.

JILL McCAFFREY has served for four years as national chairman of the Armed Forces Emergency Services of the American Red Cross. Ms. McCaffrey also serves on the board of directors for Knollwood—the Army Distaff Hall. The former Jill Ann Faulkner, a Massachusetts native, is the wife of Barry R. McCaffrey, a member of President Bill Clinton's cabinet and director of the White House Office of National Drug Control Policy. The McCaffreys are the parents of three grown children: Sean, a major in the U.S. Army; Tara, an intensive care nurse and captain in the National Guard; and Amy, a seventh grade teacher. The McCaffreys also have two grandchildren, Michael and Jack.

Picture Credits